MR SOLUTION

Fixing things

Abdi Igeh

Contents

Acknowledgement

This book is dedicated to all the men and women who paid the ultimate price - their lives - in the struggle to rebuild and defend a badly damaged country and nation by putting the jumbled jigsaw puzzle pieces together; also, those living who showed resilience and endurance with the bravery and determination to fix it.

A few of these individuals are as follows:

Singer, actress, activist and member of parliament, the late Ms Saado Ali Warsame, a Somali - American who was killed on the 23rd of July 2014 by planned execution in broad daylight in Mogadishu, when masked men jumped out of a car and fired heavy machine guns into the car she was travelling in, killing her and all the passengers instantly.

Former government minister, mayor of Mogadishu, Mr Abdirahman Omar Osman, Somali - British who was killed on the 1st of August 2019 by a suicide bomber inside the compound of the municipality.

Ms Hodan Nalayeh, Somali – Canadian, founder of Integration T.V showing the beauty of the country and its people, who was unfortunately killed by a suicide bomber on the 12th of July 2019, while pregnant, along with her husband and 20 others in the port city of Kismaayo.

Ms Almas Elman, Somali – Canadian, killed on the 20th of November 2019 by a bullet to the head near Mogadishu airport. She was the daughter of peace activist, businessman and philanthropist Mr Elman Ali, also killed in Mogadishu in 1996, who famously coined the phrase "pick up the pen; drop the gun", so Mr AI picked up the modern-day pen, which today is a laptop, to write a little something about Mr Solution's role using many different instruments including the pen to turn a country and it's nation around to better times. It's important to acknowledge it was a team effort to bring about the much-needed changes.

The thirty thousand plus people who died in the struggle, including members of parliament, government officials, military generals such as General Dhega-badan, who led the fight to clean Mogadishu of the terrorists who controlled it, and soldiers who died defending and clearing out enemies such as the terrorist group Al-Shabaab and foreign enemies.

This is just a few of the names of those who fought in the struggle. If one tried to mention or record all their names, this book would be more than 10,000 pages long, so to spare the readers the agony of that, just a handful are mentioned.

Introduction

This book was written By Mr A. Igeh, a first-time writer, about the adventurous and sometimes dangerous six and half year's biographical journey of Mr Solution in East Africa particularly Somalia, fixing, nudging and shaping things. Everybody has a story in life to tell; this is his.

It was written in London, UK when the global pandemic of coronavirus, also known as covid-19, hit the world, so as people were hibernating, shielding or advised to stay at home to protect them against the virus, it gave Mr A Igeh the opportunity to write this factual story based on real events.

10% of all proceeds or revenues of this book will go to charities such as those building clean drinking water facilities in rural hard to reach communities, and paying the educational costs of young girls and boys in East Africa. Firstly, however, if the income from this book is successful, this will be done globally, maybe even near your village or city.

Chapter 1.
The Beginning

It was a very nice spring day approaching summertime. It's 2010, and I just bought a sandwich and a can of soft drink from a café shop in Primrose Hill after a long day working, driving people around busy London, trying to beat traffic, with a terribly embarrassing back spasm for a 32-year-old which was troubling me enormously.

I parked the car and decided to have lunch in the park and get some fresh air, so I sat on the park bench watching the view of marvellous-looking London, feeling fed up with lots.

Suddenly, I made a decision; enough was enough. Time I did something about all that was bothering me and troubling Somalia and East Africa.

I remembered my early beginnings, happy times playing in the green country fields with my nomadic family who farmed hundreds of camels, sheep, goats and cows, and a time as an 8-year-old when I was running through the middle of a war between rebels and government forces, warning and evacuating the village, moving my family out of harm's way, gathering livestock, and informing people in the evening that the village can be returned to after the day that military forces occupied it. This was all done successfully while shells and heavy machine guns, being fired by both sides, were flying above me.

I have always kept up to date with current affairs in Somalia and the Somali people in East Africa as that's where I was born and where I spent my early childhood years.

The night before, I had watched this Somali-speaking TV station with the evening news of events in Somalia. It was quite negative with saddening reports coming out of Somalia. The headline was 20 to 30 dead in a day of deadly clashes between Somali warlords in the Somali capital Mogadishu.

This was very demoralising to me and to every person with a conscience and respect for human life. Being a smoker, I sat back, took a puff of the cigarette I had been smoking after lunch and thought, 'I know what is good about Somalia and the Somali people, also I know what went wrong and is still going wrong; therefore we could fix this and the sooner we get to work the better for all'.

I got a call from a friend who informed me that there was a party being held at the weekend and it's to celebrate Somalia's 50-year independence party. This was the year 2010. I said, "Put me down on the list – I am coming."

A day or two before the party, after a long day driving around London, I visited a shop in Shoreditch which sells national flags of the world and various other goods East

London to purchase over 500 of the national flag of Somalia along with 1 British flag.

The stock was loaded into the back of my seven-seater car, a Space Cruiser, and two of the flags were attached to the front of the car like a diplomat's car.

I drove to a Somali restaurant in East London where most of the regular customers are from East Africa, particularly northern Somalia, who's political clansmen in the country have formed an administration seeking to become a separate entity from the rest of Somalia.

This was due to previous political grievances, political opportunists and some businessmen who have looted national assets and turned them into private businesses and they have become multi-millionaires very quickly by paying no taxes.

Some of the usual suspects saw me park outside while they were chatting and smoking. An intense debate started, with some calling me a traitor, but some wanting to purchase a flag from me, so I started selling them for £5 each.

Months earlier, there was a terrible drought which affected Somalia and the horn of Africa, killing thousands of people and destroying agriculture and livestock.

The UK-based Aljazeera television network did a report on the Somali community's response to the drought. Mr Solution brought them to this particular coffee shop in Mile End Road, East London, where his passionate message, along with others, was aired in the report.

The weekend arrived and myself and several friends went to the independence party. There were two parties at different locations next to each other in West London, one celebrating the 26th of June, the day the national flag was first hoisted in the north of the country, and the other celebrating the 1st of July which is the official national independence and unification date of Somalia.

I went to the first party with a pair of small boxing gloves with the national flag on them that were hanging from the mirror inside my car. This party was about the 26th of June, the day the national flag was first raised in northern Somalia. There were a few singers on the stage and around 10 to 15 people attending.

The singers were the new breed of performers, quite amateurish; however, two classic Somali women folksingers, born in the north, who used to be members of the national Waaberi band, based in the capital, were sitting backstage looking quite demoralised at the whole thing.

I was smoking a cigarette and greeted them with respect. One of the old legendary singers asked me for a cigarette, then said, "I cannot believe we have been asked to perform at this level", as she was astonished at the type of party she had been asked to perform at.

Previously, in the glory days, they had been paid fantastic salaries from the Department of Culture and Information. They were performing in the national theatre in Mogadishu, Somalia, touring the world playing in prestigious events and venues.

I talked with a few of the attendees, some were familiar girls, who started asking about the flag I was waving around. I informed them, "It's the flag which was raised on the day you are celebrating in northern Somalia half a century ago; it's also the national flag of the country".

I invited them to join me at the second party just before I left.

At the second party, there were between 100 and 150 attendees but the mood and music were not right. I and my friends paid the entry fees, then as my friends entered, I went outside to get the black bag holding 250+ Somalia flags. Upon entry, I gave one to each of the doormen and the receptionist, who were all happy with the gifts.

I started giving a flag to each person, particularly all the pretty girls. The DJ saw what was happening and played K'naan's "Waving Flags" song from the world cup. The place erupted and everybody was happy waving their flags.

The party organiser approached me and bought me a drink. He said, "You have just lit up the party and stopped a possible fight breaking out between some of these young party-goers who do not know how to have a good time." He offered to give me some money as his guests had doubled in number since I did this, but I said, "No thanks, I am just glad everybody is having a good time and feeling patriotic with love and peace in the venue".

I left the party and drove my friends home. They also had a good time, particularly one who was an extreme tribalist guy. I noticed he took some of the flags inside and started distributing them, and, in the process, got a dance and a girl's phone number.

Chapter 2.
Getting Involved

This is where Mr Solution becomes active on social media and started doing interviews on Somali television networks on the current war erupting in Mogadishu and various parts of the country.

The first interview was on the Somali channel, which is a live evening broadcast from a studio in North West London.

I arrived at the building which houses various Somali satellite T.V channels, privately owned by individuals and organisations from Somalia. I had driven 2 members of the Somali community from East London to Wembley, North West London. They are Somali nationals from northern Somalia, a region called Somaliland, and are political activists who wanted to separate certain provinces in the north from the rest of the country. They have a separatist agenda and have come to visit a T.V. channel which propagates this separatist message to those who believe in it.

The two activists, a male and a female, had specifically asked me to drive them here as they knew I had created a political party called xisbiga shacabka Somalia (XSS), which means people's party of Somalia. They also knew me as being a young influential man, also from the north of the country, who openly and strongly has opinions on a union's policies on Somalia which were opposing their ideas and goals.

They viewed me as a political threat unless they could change my political opinions and activities and maybe convince me to join their bandwagon.

On this trip, it was planned for me to appear on this separatist T.V with them and promote their programmes coming up in London.

However, once we entered the building housing the Somali satellite T.V stations and my passengers entered the studio rented by the separatist T.V channel, I turned around and explored the other stations housed there which were on 2 floors next to each other.

There was a T.V studio called the Somali channel and they had planned to air a live afternoon programme, directly to Mogadishu, about the deadly fighting within the city by Somali warlords and tribal militias vying for control of the city.

The planned guest was unavailable or late, so one of the producers and a cameraman approached me, making enquiries. We started having a brief conversation about Somalia and what was happening; they seemed impressed with my Somali language and knowledge of current affairs in the country.

The producer said, "Would you like to appear on the afternoon live broadcast to Somalia and Somalis globally, with your opinion on the current situation"? I said, "Yes" and I was quickly sat down in front of the camera. Then he said, "We are live in 2 minutes". I was curious and looking around this small room turned into a studio, with a chair and table, thinking, 'Ok, let's do this'.

He said "TOOS", meaning straight in the national language, and the interviewer asked me, "What would you like to say to the people of Somalia, particularly citizens in the capital where there has been intense fighting in recent days with the loss of hundreds of lives?"

I paused for a second then said, "I would like to send a warm peaceful message to the people of Somalia firstly. Secondly, this message is to the people of Mogadishu; stop whatever you're doing for 5 minutes, look in front of you, look to your right, look to your left and look behind you. Look what you have done and are currently doing to the capital of our country and all that is within it. What you will see is death and destruction of your city and people. It's easy to destroy but much harder to build. You have learned how to be destructive to each other and destroy the most beautiful capital city in the world. Today, you must stop and learn to be peaceful, dynamic and build your city and each other."

He thanked the viewers and said, "salamu aleykum", which means 'peace be on you' in the Arabic language.

The cameraman and producers thanked me, we exchanged contact information and I went to the other studio where the 2 people who travelled with me were giving leaflets about their up and coming event to the programme-makers.

"Are you finished?" I asked. "Work is waiting for me." The male said, "Where have you been? We have been asking for you." "Exploring the busy building," I replied. He smiled with a look of disappointment then said, "Ok, fine. You can leave. We are going to be here for a while".

I left and started my night shift working in central London. I remember feeling quite optimistic and proud of what I had just done.

The following day, the war raging in the Somali capital stopped for a long period of time, and in the coming days and weeks, there was peace and quiet in the city for a change. Contact or dialogue between the warring sides was reported.

I quickly realised my live message to the people could have been the key to pausing the conflict, bringing peace and making the guns silent even if it was only for a while.

The reason for this was that I was different with how the message I sent on T.V. sounded to the people, as the public viewed me as a straight-talking, honest young man without any hidden agenda, independent from bias to all parties involved in the conflict. Also, there was a big difference in age and background, such as place of birth and clan, and political ideology compared to the usual politicians, warlords, religious and tribal leaders the people were used to seeing on T. V and radios.

A week or so later, Mr Solution started having meetings with the Somali community from the Diaspora in various parts of London, where a diverse community from all parts of Somalia had settled and made it their home since arriving in the United Kingdom, some as early as the 1960s.

These meetings were normally informal and took place in Somali restaurants and cafés. Mr Solution did this purposefully, in order to gauge the mood and understand further real issues existing in the country generally, particularly the regions where these individuals originated from.

One member of the Somali community said, "I cannot see peace or prosperity breaking out in Somalia while blatant discrimination and crimes are committed by ignorant groups against my people". This was against certain members of his community or tribe unjustly, purely, as he said, in ignorance.

Mr Solution was aware of this as, when he was a young boy growing up in Somalia, his grandfather, who was rich in livestock compared to most, used to give away some livestock and allow free drinking from wells to certain members of Somali families who lived inside the villages or near his home.

These families were mainly skilled tradespeople who used to make shoes, clothes, pots, knives and other metal objects, while the majority of the population were nomadic Somalis who travelled with their livestock seeking green pastures.

Mr Solution remembered seeing the dead body of a man from this particular tribe, who was killed along with twenty plus other Somalis from different communities when fighting broke out between government forces and armed rebels fighting to overthrow the military regime which had ruled Somalia for a long time in 1989.

This man was known to Mr Solution as he used to make his shoes, household cookery tools and special milking bowls used to milk the camels the family had.

Mr Solution realised, after research and common sense, that unfortunately, it was true that these minority tribes were discriminated against purely because they have a different profession of work compared to the majority of other communities, so, basically, it was a class issue. Discrimination or racism, such as not allowing boys and girls from these tribes to marry girls and boys from the majority nomadic tribes, was due to fake propaganda; class superiority issues existed.

Mr Solution knew these unjustly discriminated tribes or groups were extremely important to the national economy, just like the farmers of livestock, fishermen, and agricultural farmers.

Mr Solution also realised that these groups, along with others, had become fertile ground for terrorist groups such as Al-Shabaab militants, who have caused death and destruction in Somalia by manipulating and using their grievances to join them.

This is where Mr Solution promised this gentleman, with whom he had been having an intense conversation on Somali affairs, that he would fix this injustice as he agreed with him that it was complete nonsense, ignorance and fake propaganda and this should not exist anymore in Somalia or anywhere else in the world.

From this day onwards, Mr Solution started a campaign for equality and inclusion of all marginalised groups in all sectors of government, social and economic life, therefore, ideas and policies were created to make sure they were represented and respected just like all the others.

He started by ordering some of his own family in Somalia, who were experiencing severe drought due to irregular seasonal rains, to use the funds that Mr Solution was sending in the form of money remittances to purchase truckloads of fresh drinking water from the district capital city to rural families, then livestock was also to be given, first to the villagers and then to marginalised families.

Certain family members were reluctant to do this and had very weak excuses but Mr Solution threatened to stop the money being remitted immediately if those conditions were not carried out.

The family members came to their senses and agreed to provide free drinking water to the people or communities Mr Solution had mentioned, after all, this was what our grandfather used to do also. This was the first step in bringing consciousness and change within communities, starting with his own family, by starting with this small gesture.

Changes and political representation of these unjustly discriminated groups were implemented shortly afterwards when Mr Solution recruited 4 central committee members of the newly formed political party from individuals within these tribes. Because of this small initial action, it was then followed by recommendations to the federal government of Somalia in the form of government ministers and committee members to be appointed from these tribes as it was a good political policy.

The Somali region of Ethiopia was ushering in a rebirth in terms of administration and authority due to the new constitution of Ethiopia and political progress taking shape in their brotherly neighbour Somalia. The region's leader was then Mr Abdi Omar of the Somali people's Ethiopian Democratic Party.

The Somali region's president organised the "wedding of the century" as they called it, which was to bring 100 girls and 100 men from the discriminated groups and other Somali clans/ tribes to marry each other.

The regional administrators would pay for all wedding costs, build a fully furnished 3 or 4-bedroom house for each couple, and provide a cash sum to each couple to set up a business or create employment for them.

This project was a great success as it was witnessed by Mr Solution, who was a guest in one of the happy couples' homes in Jigjiga city in Ethiopia, on his way to London via Addis Ababa. The happy couple did this as they knew Mr Solution was the main instigator of the idea behind this originally and it was only right that they did this, as the man was passing through Ethiopia after a gruelling few years in Somalia on the way to London.

Some days, Mr Solution was driving around south London, in areas such as Battersea, Streatham, Lewisham and the Old Kent Road. Other days he worked in areas in the north, east and west of London such as Tottenham, Fulham, Hackney, Whitechapel, Newham, Southall and Hayes. This was all done while working around London as a self-employed person while also networking, and conducting research on Somali affairs.

A week later, Mr Solution decided to create a national political party in Somalia to be called the "people's party of Somalia" or xisbiga shacabka Somalia (XSS) in the national language of Somalia.

This was done after meeting women's groups, Somalia elders, university students and young professional Somalis from the Diasporas who all expressed a desire to see the flourishing democracy, which once existed in Somalia, return after a 49-year absence.

Within two weeks of Mr Solution conceiving the vision, the idea was put to work. The name, logo and website of the people's party of Somalia were planned, and a creative art and design person was found to design a unique logo for the party. Information and ideas were supplied to the designer, who produced a colourful unique party logo.

A web design company was found which would build the party website with the policy and information on it, and Mr Solution was issued a logon by the company so he could upload pictures, party policies, and party materials to raise funds and share contact information.

T-shirts, mugs, posters and flags with the party logo on them were printed for promotional purposes. A meeting for the creation of the party's central committee was held in London and, via telephone conference, 23 members were selected, of whom 7 were women, which amount to 30% of the central committee.

The party leader and chairman was then selected. Mr Solution was chosen in a quick vote since he was the party founder and also the main policy-maker.

A second T.V interview was held, and this time Mr Solution was interviewed by a presenter nicknamed Tolwaye on the Somali channel again. The interview was 57 minutes long to be precise.

The interview took place in the same studio, 3 months after the last T.V broadcast message was done, after Mr Solution returned from a hajj pilgrimage to Mecca.

After introductions, the first question the interviewer asked was, "What do you think Somalia needs right now?" Mr S replied, "A new constitution which protects the country and people from harm, also keeping the country and citizens together, making the law superior".

The reason Mr Solution said this first was because the first Somalia constitution, made and passed in 1960 after independence and unification, had political issues which needed clarification. This was urgent in order for building a new state to really commence.

One of the key issues or mistakes was that it did not mention where Somalia's land borders actually ran, and, because of this reason, Somalia and Somalis had security issues and political and economic interference from its neighbours such as Ethiopia, Kenya and Djibouti.

The Somali people also had the idea for a long time that all land inhabited by Somalis, even inside international borders of neighbouring countries, constituted a territory of Somalia.

Some months later, a new federal constitution was drafted by the transitional federal government with assistance from international partners.

In the summertime, there was a meeting, held in Swiss Cottage Marriott Hotel in London, to consult the citizens from the diasporas on the new constitutions which had been drafted and, an invitation to attend was received. The meeting was organised by members of the transitional Somali federal government, and certain technocrats had been given the job of drafting and consulting on the new constitution.

Although extremely difficult for some citizens to accept, Mr Solution proposed we accept and concede the old mentality while attending the conference, and the new constitution should clearly stipulate that Somalia consists of the northern and southern territory, 18 provinces, which gained independence from Britain and Italy and unification on the 1st of July 1960, only with their own created borders.

This decision was very bitter for some Somalis to accept at the time as it was conceding large territories of Somali-inhabited land to neighbouring countries, which they were part of legally whether they like it or not. Mr Solution's decision or advice was the necessary medicine and the solution to rebuilding Somalia, also strengthening the Somalis who were part of neighbouring countries, giving them the opportunity to fully participate in all social, economic and political institutions of the countries in which they were legally citizens.

Mr Solution sent emails and liaised with the individuals who were tasked with drafting the new constitution, encouraging them to seriously consider this and include this, however much opposition there was, as this would make the path of state rebuilding easier for many reasons.

This was a key question and important response from Mr Solution, as this kick-started a political process urgently needed at a crucial moment.

An impassioned rallying article called "Home is where the heart is", written and published in various websites and social media pages by the party leader, created a blueprint of what needed to happen in order to move the country and people forward from the terrible circumstances faced at that time.

The article looked at the success the country had achieved from independence in 1960 and the grave failures which had occurred also.

The main point of the article argued that what unites the people and country, such as history, ethnicity, language, religion, economy and birth, is greater than what divides them and a national peace conference, which was needed to reconcile and reconnect it, would map out a way forward.

The article was published in various Somali-orientated websites, forums, the XSS party website and various social media pages, including those of Mr Solution, as this was the time when the internet was growing at a rapid pace, creating spaces where people could interact. It was also shown to members of the British government at the time by party founder and leader, Mr Solution, after meeting in London and enjoying a conversation about political affairs in the UK and Somalia.

Positive feedback was received which resulted in the UK government holding a conference on Somalia on the 23rd of February 2012, in Lancaster House, London. The venue was where the name Somalia had been first written and signed as an independent sovereign country on the 26th of June 1960.

More than 50 delegates from various parts of Somalia, who each controlled little bits of the inland space of the country, attended and this was the first time they had all met under the umbrella of a national peace conference on Somalia in almost 20 years.

Somali delegates had the opportunity to hold this Somalia national peace conference inside the country as citizens ideally wanted, but unfortunately, these Somali administrators failed miserably due to insecurities, lack of leadership, self-interest and political will.

The conference was held and co-chaired by the then British Prime Minister, David Cameron, along with the federal transition of Somalia's then-president, Sheik Sharrif, and Prime Minister Dr Abdiweli Gaas. Also attending were the provincial leaders of various parts of the country such as Somaliland, Puntland, Galmudug, Ahlu Sunna Waljama'a, NGOs, various diplomats, and heads of state of many countries including the African Union, United Nations and the Turkish government.

Mr Solution started interacting with members of the Turkish community as he lived and went to school where there was a large Turkish community in the UK as a young boy.

Restaurants and mosques were places where connections and conversation with members of the British Turkish community would take place in East London.

Mr Solution understood that the foreign policy of Turkey was changing to a more global policy of trade and cooperation and this could be an important partner to Somalia to rebuild the nation and economy after years of decline and destruction.

The day before the conference was held, Mr Solution was telephoned by the Somali channel to do an interview as a political analyst on the Somalia conference. Mr Solution accepted, arrived at the studio and various questions were asked of him by the programme presenter, such as what would be on the agenda at the conference and the possible outcomes.

Mr Solution explained that piracy in the Somali seas, security building and cooperation, fighting terrorism, building government institutions and facilities, progress on reconciliation, peace-building and democracy would certainly be on the agenda.

At the end of the meeting, for the interest of the people, some of the outcomes were mentioned, along with advice to the Somali attendees, such as speaking in the national Somali language when making speeches or statements at the conference.

The famous Somali artist/cartoonist Amir Arts, who lives in Canada, published a cartoon sketch which showed the Somali dignitaries boarding a plane on their way to the Somali conference with 2 characters saying, "Speak Somali to each other and when delivering speeches at the meetings".

The Somalia transitional president at the time gave his speech in the Arabic language, while his prime minister delivered his speech in English. The regional leader of the northern part of Somalia called Somaliland also used English; a foreign language.

When visiting Somali restaurants and cafés frequented by the Diasporas community in the U.K, certain members of the community informed Mr Solution, "We watched your interview and you are true patriotic

Somali man, better than these guys attending the conference who didn't even have the confidence to speak in the national language of our country".

Chapter 3.
The Peace Cup, Fixing the Capital Mogadishu

This is where Mr Solution left London and landed in the Somali capital, Mogadishu, on a sunny afternoon.

Mr Solution said, "Fixing a country is like building a strong house". There is a Somali proverb which says, "haan gunta ayaa laga tolaa", meaning things are built or joined together from the bottom up; the first part is having the vision to build the house, then making a plan to build this house and finally, gathering resources to start the construction.

It's crucially important that the work of building a nation and solving its long-standing issues, faced by both country and people, is done more from inside, while good work has been done from outside already in the past years, but it was a top-down approach, so building from the bottom up and top-sealing it permanently in the middle would be a new approach that could work tremendously quickly at fixing things, so, therefore, Mr Solution decided it was a good time to go inside Somalia and distribute and plant the seeds of peace, hope, reconciliation, unity, government institution-building, security, economy and sports.

At that time, Mr Solution was beginning to understand that the problems of any country and people will not magically fix themselves but can only be solved by someone who understands the complexity of the situation with supportive attractive cooperation from international partners.

It was the 18th of August, 2012. Mr Solution had purchased a plane ticket to Mogadishu, the Somali capital.

The flight left London around midnight and arrived around 09:30 in Dubai airport to catch a connecting flight to Somalia in the morning.

There were around two and a half hours left before the connecting flight left, which gave him time to browse through the airport shops on the way to the boarding gate. Slightly lost as some of the signs were unclear, he asked for directions from airport employees who pointed the direction out with hesitation. He finally arrived at the boarding gate after avoiding a few slightly shady-looking Somalis asking weird questions regarding where in Somalia he was travelling to and why these chaps are from northern Somalia by their accents.

Reached the boarding gate after worrying slightly about the time due to the gate not been found swiftly, he sat down in the waiting area. There was this tall Somali man with shades and scars on his face. He said, "I am a businessman from the Bakara market, Mogadishu, and you?" Mr Solution said, "I am a Somali citizen, returning from Europe, travelling to the capital Mogadishu."

He boarded the plane, a short flight of around 3 hours which landed in Berbera airport, northern Somalia, to drop off and pick up passengers then continue to Mogadishu. Some airport staff boarded the plane as some passengers were getting off here. One of them looked at Mr Solution as if he knew him or wanted to ask something but then they got off, and the plane reloaded its passengers and cargo, taking off for its final destination - Mogadishu.

The plane landed around 3 pm in Mogadishu airport, now called Aden Adde airport (AAA), after rebuilding by the Turkish government's development agencies.

The airport lies by the Indian Ocean and, as the plane approaches the landing strip, the view from the plane is magnificent. Mr Solution has arrived, for the first time, in the capital of Somalia. The sun is shining and it's very hot. It's the 19th of August 2019.

Mr Solution, who initially joined the national citizen's queue for immigration, was asked to join the queue for people who were travelling with a foreign passport, after protesting furiously with Somali immigration staff about this decision as he had completely forgotten he was travelling with a European passport and not a Somali national passport.

Mr Solution apologised and calmly re-joined the non-nationals queue for immigration once the reason for this was explained to him by airport staff, although he was feeling slightly annoyed he was not in the queue with nationals.

On first impressions, the airport looked like it needed a lot of refurbishment and rebuilding after years of war and neglect. Mr Solution received his suitcase after paying an airport baggage-handler to retrieve it and take it to a waiting car outside as there was chaos due to lack of organisation or management.

"How is work and life?" asked Mr Solutions to the airport bag-handler. "It's good when the work is available. It's not much but it pays for my family's food and kids' school fees," says the bag man.

The tall Somali businessman from the Bakara market and Mr Solution exchanged contact numbers as he was also leaving the airport at that time. The tall scar-faced man gave his Mogadishu phone number as Mr Solution did not have a local mobile number and international roaming was not working in Somalia yet.

Mr Solution lit a cigarette outside the terminal after a long journey without it. Looking around, the sky was completely blue, the airport was located on the edge of the Indian Ocean and it was all blue, and the national flag of Somalia was hoisted outside the old busy airport, waving from side to side.

Outside the heavily guarded airport, on a dusty road with sand from the beach, he walked towards the car which had been waiting to pick up Mr Solution. A very dark-skinned, clean-shaven man waved and said, "Keep coming!" Handshakes and hugs were exchanged and bags were loaded into the boot of the Toyota. "I am Layli," said the man. "We have been waiting for your landing. How was the flight?" "Yes, it was long and tiring but generally good, and I am very happy and excited to be home in the capital Mogadishu."

They started driving down Airport Road towards the Zobe roundabout, heading for the hamar weyne (the old city) district where Layli's family, particularly his father who was also from the U.K and Mogadishu, had a bedroom fixed up ready for Mr Solution to stay in.

Since it was the first time Mr Solution had ever visited the capital, he took his phone out and started taking pictures and recording videos of the views. The driver, Layli, called somebody and said in the Somali language, "I want a head; which do you have, black or white?" As his phone was already out while taking pictures, Mr Solution started to record the conversation the driver was having and was completely baffled by the whole thing. It was worrying Mr Solution a little as it made him think maybe this man wanted to cook a human head to eat, and he hoped it was not his. "Did you get what you wanted?" asked Mr Solution while recording it all. "Yes, I have this terrible flu and wanted a goat head to give to the housemaid to cook and make spicy soup for me."

"Ok, hopefully, it should clear that out," said Mr solution, but he really found the whole thing unusual due to Mr Solution being from the north of Somalia, where livestock was in abundance and men never eat the head or certain other parts of animals; only fine-cut pieces of the carcass were permitted to men.

Driving through a busy unorganised market, the car stopped outside an apartment block in the old city. Suitcases were unloaded and carried up 2 flights of stairs and the lady of the house opened the door and greeted us. Mr solution entered and embraced the father of Layli. "Salaam, uncle; nice to finally meet you. How are you? Your lovely daughter sends her love and she has also given me a package to give you." His daughter in the UK was the one who had made the connection with this family possible as they lived close by in London.

The old man of the house showed Mr Solution the room which had been organised for his stay. "This is your room. Relax and rest; I am sure you had a long journey over here as I make the same journey regularly. As you already know, I am both a Mogadishu and a London resident."

Mr Solution had a shower and found Layli was in his room watching some premiership football via a Somali satellite T.V. This was a pleasant surprise to Mr Solution who was a massive football supporter. "Who is playing?" asked Mr Solution. "It's 2 teams from the EPL, mid-table stuff."

Layli said, "Get dressed if you want to go to the market in hamar weyne with me." "Yes, great, give me two minutes, man".

After a short walk, we arrived in this busy market full of traders and shoppers. There were fruit and vegetable sellers, clothes sellers, tailors, many exchange men, khat (this is a potent stimulant plant whose leaves Somali men chew to keep them awake and high for a long period of time), and sweet sellers mainly selling halwa and various Somali-style biscuits.

First stop, the money exchange. Mr solution gave Layli two hundred US dollars, but Layli gave 150 US dollars back and said, "This is all we need for now." Purchases were made from the sweet trader of 2 kilos of halwa, then, after some banter and haggling, the juice and ice seller was approached and a bag of ice and different types of juices were bought. Then finally, they visited the khat dealer and 30 dollars' worth of the best was purchased, as advised by Layli, then they returned to the flat.

"Dinner is served!" said Layli's father. Four of us sat around the table as a bowl of hand wash was circulated before tucking into the food.

The housemaid, who was also a relative of the tenants, brought the food out and we served each other a plateful.

After dinner, Mr Solution and Layli sat in the living room watching football while chewing the potent khat leaves imported daily from Kenya to Somalia.

Mr Solution heard some gunshots nearby and asked Layli, "What's that about?" Layli said, "Don't worry, man, let's return to our conversation. I think it's some idiots from the neighbourhood who are high and idiotic; they are not the real deal".

"I hear you, man, where was I at?" I then opened the HP laptop I had brought with me and wrote the title of the important plan or blueprint called "**The Peace Cup**".

A week passed and Mr Solution moved to a hotel named Wardheere (the long-distance news) on the main road called the hart or maka almukaramma in more recent times due to another hotel located there.

The hotel was one of the few newly built hotels in Mogadishu. All the hotel's facilities were fairly modern or newly installed. Due to its good location, facilities and security arrangements, this hotel was full with government officials, new and old parliamentary candidates, presidential candidates, tribal elders or customary leaders who had been tasked with selecting members of parliament from their respected clans or regions, tourists, business people, and Somali expatriates from all over the world, particularly Europe, the USA and Canada.

Mr Solution checked in with the receptionist who advised that the room booked over the phone was ready. The hotel receptionist, also the front of house manager, who was a man, informed Mr Solution that he was also from the UK after viewing the passport which was taken and kept in the hotel safe upon check-in, along with any other valuables the guests may wish to hand in.

Mr Solution was shown to a second-floor room with a double bed, table, remote-controlled air conditioner, and en suite shower/bathroom. Mr Solution declined and asked if he could show him a simpler room? "Yes, there is a single bed-only room upstairs on the 3rd floor but it will be the same price, just so you know." The room on the third floor was viewed. "Perfect. Just what I needed, a single bed with a view of the displaced people's camp outside," said Mr Solution. "I will take it."

This was done deliberately by Mr Solution so he did not forget for long the main reason why he came to Somalia, which was to help and change the situation of all, including the displaced people that needed to see better days ahead in the future.

The hotel worker was slightly baffled by this but said, "Ok, here are the keys to your room; enjoy. Please drop the key off at reception when you are leaving the building and collect it on your return."

Once showered, the luggage was unpacked. One bag, full of t-shirts with the name and logo of Xisbiga shacabka Somalia printed on it, was opened. Mr Solution wore a t-shirt to the hotel lobby to have afternoon tea and snacks with some friends and members of the party who had arrived from other cities and neighbouring countries.

Other hotel guests and visitors were also downstairs, as it was a busy time of the day. In the hotel lobby were 4 young men who had been supporters of the political organisation founded by Mr Solution. Two were Mogadishu residents who were sitting at a table waiting to meet Mr Solution.

Warm greetings were exchanged - "Really nice to meet you in person finally," said one of the young men wearing an oversized suit jacket. "Likewise, my brothers," said Mr Solution.

"Is that the people's party t-shirt you are wearing?" asked one of the men named Warfaa. "Yes. I have plenty upstairs for each of you and some for you to distribute to your friends.

Follow me to my room to collect some now." Upstairs, a t-shirt was given to each one, plus some extra to give out, and then they returned to order tea and coffee from the bar.

Walking around were these old tribal clan leaders and others, all scrambling to be part of the new parliament that was being selected for the up and coming people's parliament (golaha shacabka). They were all looking at us with these bright-coloured political party t-shirts.

One gentleman came over and said, "You young men are miles ahead of everyone here in Somalia. Political parties are unheard of here as we have not reached that yet. Are you from outside Somalia just returning?"

Mr Solution was, but these young party members were from Mogadishu and wanted to see the democratic political process return since it had been absent since 1969. "Yes, that's right; we, the young Somalis, are a majority in Somalia, but are not represented or valued as we should be due to conflict or purposely being ignored and no opportunity is been given in the political decision-making process. That's why some are migrating away, and some are joining terrorist groups like Al-Shabaab due to these frustrations," replied one of the young men.

"Yes, that's right. You heard the man, and don't call him kid, Mister, as I am sure you would not like him calling you old man," said Mr Solution.

A pause and a laugh, then he said, "We don't mind being called old men. As you can see, we, the elders, are the decision-makers here, forming the people's parliament we are most respected and listened to." "Mister, if you don't know, the most valuable asset a country has is its young people who have the energy, ideas and strength to defend and develop their country," said Mr Solution.

Smiles and handshakes were given between us and the old tribal chief, who said, "The truth is, we need you guys as we have been making a mess of things for a long time and it's properly your time to lead and change things with new ideas, but can you take it off us as we aren't going to hand it to you?"

"Time will tell, chief, but we are very confident of marking that positive change. However, chief, all good citizens of our country must work together to achieve this, not against each other," said Mr Solution.

The chief nodded and returned to his table. Mr Solution said to the young men around the table, "Do you see how this tribal leader acknowledged you, had a proper debate when he sees you are working together as an organisation with your party t-shirts on?" "We did notice actually," said Warfaa. "I think some elders are already getting worried they may become redundant or retired by us. As you know, in Somalia, there is no retirement age."

Contact numbers were exchanged and a meeting with some local poets and the national youth organisation, who are having an event in their temporary head office, was arranged for the following day after the meeting again.

Mr Solution went to inspect the hotel fully, such as all the entries and exits to the building for security reasons, while also looking for the laundry people. At the back of the hotel building, there was the kitchen and two exit and entry doors, which Mr Solution noticed. He asked the chef where the laundryman was, then thanked him for the delicious steak he had cooked for him. The chef explained that the laundry was on the roof of the building.

Mr Solution walked up the stairs of the 3-floor hotel, inspecting each floor on the way up to the roof, meeting people along the way. Then finally, the roof; wow, fantastic! 'What a view of Mogadishu and the Indian Ocean,' thought Mr Solution.

"Hello, laundryman. I am a resident of the hotel and would like some clothes washed, please. shall I bring them up or will you collect them from me in the room?" "Leave them outside your door. I will be there shortly to take them."

Back downstairs, Mr Solution met these young Somali returnees, from various places around the world, having a conversation about their experiences of being back in Mogadishu.

One of them introduced himself as Shire daone from the statehouse, a very interesting guy from Canada who introduced Mr Solution to various people in Mogadishu while there. The other was the director of an organisation called Fighting Tribalism, based in the UK, but the truth was that this guy, I learned later, had other agendas in addition to fighting tribalism, as some of his actions and behaviours indicated.

Also present was a young lady called Araweelo, named after the strong queen who ruled Somalia around 5000 years ago, who was known to remove men's testicles as part of her reign. "I am Mr Solution, founder and party chairman of the people's party of Somalia. I have travelled from the UK to Mogadishu. Here is my card. I will write my mobile number on the back. There is this event tomorrow, organised by the national youth association, with national poets. I hope you can attend; just call me."

The following day, Mr Solution asked for a taxi, so the front of house manager made a call and said "Biibaye is coming; he is a good safe driver. You and all your friends should use him. He is outside the front door now. Thanks; see you later in the evening hopefully."

On leaving the hotel, Mr Solution noticed two ladies, sitting in the corner of the lobby, wearing traditional colourful dresses. A smile and waves were exchanged. Mr Solution remembered that these were the same ladies who joined his breakfast table the day before, deliberately, as there were plenty of available tables. They had asked various questions such as what was he doing here in Mogadishu? And how long was he here for? etc.

One of the ladies said, "We are from Hargeisa. We are here on business while also visiting properties my family has here".

This place mentioned is the second largest major city in Somalia, located in the northern part of Somalia, locally administered by the self-declared autonomous region called Somaliland, which, after the overthrow of the military dictatorship in 1991, and ensuing anarchy, tribal war and looting, formed a regional government who basically was controlled by tribal alliances, former rebels, military leaders from the fallen regime, and businessmen who have benefitted from the looting and chaos since 1991.

Mr Solution was born in the northern part of Somalia; however, he did not agree with the political stances or position of the leaders in northern Somalia. Because of this, some members of that region's regime had tried some very underhand tactics and attempts to discredit and harm Mr Solution's political activities using any means possible, so he was very weary of these ladies.

Some political foes believed women were Mr Solution's weak area, as, when younger, Mr Solution was a ladies' man and could not say no to a pretty woman, so using these women was something Mr Solution was expecting, therefore, the man must be disciplined and not get caught napping.

By taxi, he arrived at the national youth association's main hall where a performance with singers and musicians had already begun, the organisers and some of the guests welcomed Mr Solution, along with introductions about their role in nation and government-building.

Mr Solution was impressed that a female was head of the national youth organisation as he had been championing female participation in political, economic, and social affairs in Somalia while abroad, as was clearly stated in past TV interviews, articles written and also the major inclusion of females in the people's party of Somalia's membership and leadership.

A poet and activist, who had also travelled from the UK, was sitting next to Mr Solution as the performers and speakers did their stuff on the little crowded stage. The young political activists called SSC, from northern Somalia, who were also strongly pro-unity and reconciliation of Somalia, were present, sitting in the corner. Introductions were made then words of encouragement were spoken, then pictures of them were taken together.

The few people from the Somali Diaspora attending met outside the hall at the end. Some pictures were taken and phone contacts and meeting points were arranged for later at the village restaurant owned by a returnee chef who cooked fine tasty modernised traditional cuisine.

They had arranged for a taxi to take them back to the hotel, but changed their minds and decided to walk back.

It was hot and humid to some but Mr Solution was basking in the glorious sunshine then stopped at a mobile cold drink-makers and ice cream-sellers then ordered a mango and papaya juice with ice for himself and his friend from the event.

A conversation took place with the local residents and traders about life in Mogadishu. One said, "We have seen worse times here; there is some sort of normality returning. I think the people's brains are starting to re-function." "How is business for you"? "These days, it's getting much better as there is more peace and security in the city, which means more customers moving around from place to place and occasionally stopping at my juice bar, like yourselves."

They continued walking as they were approaching the hotel, armed men were outside the entrances and some hotel guests were sitting outside some smoking, others drinking hot drinks and there were the two girls from northern Somalia with the colourful flowing dresses who had shown an unusual interest in Mr Solution's activities. "Hello, ladies. Enjoying the fine weather we are having here today?"

The big tall curvy one said, "It's always like this in Mogadishu; nothing new. What's it like where you came from?"

"Well, it's always changing. We get a variety in the weather patterns over there. We also like talking about the weather, that's properly why I mentioned it. Ok, ladies, I am sweating quite heavily. As you can see, my shirt is drenched. Must dash to the shower to freshen up for you fine ladies with all that nice UUNSI smell blowing from your direction. I will be back shortly".

UUNSI is made from frankincense mixed with perfumes then cooked in a pot with fire by Somali women, then finally burnt on charcoal giving smoky fumes to make their bodies and clothes smell good.

He looked back and one of the girls looked at him with a warm smile; the other gazed at Mr Solution as if he was the enemy she had been sent to investigate.

Every day for the next week or so was spent travelling around the city, meeting new people, mainly to discuss the security, business and political direction of the country while eating camel meat, drinking camel milk, eating papaya fruit as a dessert or chewing the khat stimulant.

One day, Mr Solution was sitting on the hotel balcony with his laptop while writing the 12-page Peace Cup blueprint plan. Inside the hall behind is a meeting of politicians, civil society members and tribal leaders, mainly from Mogadishu. Mr Solution heard some of what was being discussed, such as past events, clan wars, killings, looting, peace-building and reconciliation.

"Enough work for today," he said. He packed up the laptop and charger. Upon re-entering and passing through the hall where the deadlocked meeting was continuing, Mr Solution greeted the table and said, "What has happened in the past has taken place in the past; it's gone. You should leave it there and make a new positive beginning together, moving forward for today and tomorrow." There was complete silence then one said, "He is absolutely right; that is what we should do".

I continued to the stairs to my room and one of the meeting attendees ran behind me and said "Mr Solution! Hold on! What is your actual name?" I smiled and said, "Mudane xaliye, as you say, is just fine." And that is how the nickname Mr Solution was given to me.

Evening time arrived, usually time for the evening prayers. Mr Solution prayed in the local mosque opposite behind some little houses, while most hotel residents who prayed performed it in the little prayer room on the roof of the hotel, followed by tea and snacks in the hotel restaurant.

There was a little restaurant which served authentic and traditional national foods, full of flavour compared to the hotel restaurant which had very little flavour or variety, although hotel guests were paying high prices to stay at this hotel. Mr Solution, who had sampled the food and drinks at this small bar-restaurant before, that evening after prayers, ordered food and drinks which came to 50,000 Somali shillings or 4 dollars. He said, "Here are 100 US dollars. Please keep the change and open an account for me as I want to eat here often instead of the hotel; your food is much better." The restaurant owner said, "Thanks, yes, sure," took my name and entered it into his book.

Returning to the hotel, the two ladies with the colourful flowing traditional dresses were sitting at the reception area watching the T.V with other guests. He quickly got changed then called the usual taxi driver to meet him outside the main hotel entrance as an evening of socialising with some fine ladies and gents working on the approaching elections had been arranged.

The car arrived on time. Driving along the road to the guest house for the meeting, which is approximately 15 minutes from the hotel, he noticed a car, which had been following them for a long time, at times coming very close.

Biibaye was a young fresh driver who was very excited with the clientele paying hard currency on a daily basis using his car, so he had not noticed the car following them but had seen that at times the car behind him had come close to hitting his car from behind.

Mr Solution told the driver to continue driving straight ahead and to pass the original address, take the next road on the right and stop there to drop him off.

The following day, Mr Solution, who had a meeting with NGOs working in the Somali capital at their compound, ordered the hotel taxi driver, Biibaye, to wait outside the front entrance but also ordered another taxi driver to wait in the little road behind the hotel near the internally displaced camps. Mr Solution left the hotel via the kitchen at the back entrance and took the waiting taxi to the meeting, but phoned Biibaye and said, "I have sent $10 to your mobile wallet now, so drive the car around the city then return to the hotel, parking in the same place as before and find out who was following you around".

Biibaye informed Mr Solution that it was the two ladies staying at the same hotel who were following him around in the other car.

The two colourfully dressed girls spying on Mr Solution had been following an empty car around Mogadishu for thirty minutes before realising it was an empty car, so when he returned to the hotel in a different car, the heavy ladies were sitting in reception. "Good evening, ladies. It's extra humid tonight, or is it me"? They replied, "We have been inside the hotel with the air conditioning on all day so we have not noticed."

I smiled then ran up the steps to the hotel room for a shower and change of clothing as a dinner party had been organised by these young returnees, mainly from Europe and Canada. The dinner was being cooked by the best Somali chef in Somalia, who had also opened 3 successful restaurants in Mogadishu.

I put on my dinner jacket with a nice colourful shirt and very nice men's cologne called VIP 212 by Carolina Herrera. On the way out of the hotel, the super heavy ladies were sitting outside at the hotel gate. "Hello again, ladies. I am off to dinner now. See you later," said Mr

Solution. "Are we not invited?" asked one of them. "Sorry, ladies, I was only informed about it at short notice by a friend who is one of the organisers."

I ordered the hotel taxi and Biibaye arrived swiftly. We drove to the restaurant where the event was being held. The whole idea of this dinner party was for Somali returnees to meet, exchange ideas and to further collaborate on working together to achieve their goals.

There were more than a hundred guests attending. The party organisers were asking for everybody to stand up when it was their turn to introduce themselves by name, say where they travelled from and their plans in Somalia while here.

Some said they were here to improve the food security of Somalia by investing, training Somali farmers by travelling throughout the country on a fact-finding mission first, some had started businesses while here, such as telecommunication companies, banks, export businesses and others were on holiday visiting families. Some said they had arrived to help and assist the Somali election process.

Finally, it was Mr Solution's turn to speak. "Salaam. Firstly, my name is Xaliye. I have travelled from the UK, and I am a man in search of his lost camels." There was a little pause and complete laughter by all attendees including Mr Solution.

" On a serious level, let me explain that Somali joke's meaning; the biggest institution which can make the large changes needed to create the right conducive environment to enable all of you to achieve your goals here is good governance and good political policies to direct the country and its people in the right direction.

I am the founder and leader of the people's party of Somalia (XSS), which is the first democratic political party to be formed since 1969, hoping to return the voice and aspirations of the people to them and you're all welcome to join." Warm applause followed then the party continued.

Mr Solution called one of the dinner party hosts and said, "Can you please fix 3 plates of food for these two young local gentlemen who have just arrived, and my driver, please?" He said, "Sorry, man, I don't know them".

Quite upset by this, Mr Solution said, "Ok, brother, no problem. I will sort these guys out, so you go do your thing".

Mr Solution got up, walked around the long square dinner table shaking hands along the way to the kitchen, where the chef who owned the hotel restaurant was, and greeted him saying, "Mohammed, the food was fantastic. Thanks again and happy to see you here in Mogadishu, fellow Londoner. I know as I was a regular customer in your restaurant in London's Hammersmith. There is my driver and 2 local guys who arrived late; can you please fix 3 plates for them?"

"Sure. I will see what's left." After the driver had eaten, followed by some drinks, we departed to the hotel around 11 pm. The following day Mr Solutions decided to visit some of the old national monuments by walking down the main central road of the city towards the radio station where an interview on the midday programme was scheduled with Mr Solution.

First stop - taaloda zeydka - it was a monument of Mohammed Abdullah Hassan on a horse but it's empty as the monument was looted during the war and anarchy after the overthrow of the long-ruling military regime.

Mr Solution climbed the big structure which the missing monument was on top of, had a picture taken by a friend and said, "Somebody has to fill the void till this monument is restored to its former glory, someday, sooner rather than later hopefully, but today it's me posing on it as the new national warrior."

The radio station was located at the house of the mothers' building. The director of the station, who is also a poet, was introduced by one of the reporters to Mr solution. After a brief discussion, the interview was conducted with questions such as 'what do you think of the capital?'

'What does your political party hope to achieve while here in Somalia?' Quick general answers were given.

There was a restaurant below the house of the mothers' building where Mr Solution decided to have lunch and coffee as it was also a restaurant owned by chef Mohamed from the previous evening. It's called "The Village".

This place was rebuilt after it had been unfortunately bombed by the Terrorist group Al-Shabaab some months before with lots of deaths, mostly of young Somali journalists from the city, some known to Mr Solution. They used to meet up at that spot to plan their day's work schedules, but that day, more than 30 died.

Sitting in the restaurant was Mr Shidde, a Somali comedy actor of recent times. Mr Solution joined him and requested his food and drinks be served at this table instead and to take the order of Mr Shidde, who said, "Thanks, but I have just eaten my lunch. Just espresso please," to the waiter.

Mr Solution tells Shidde how the comedy sketches shown on Somali satellite T.V are enjoyed by Somali people abroad, who are informed and entertained by this light comedy created in Mogadishu which shows a different perspective of real issues faced by ordinary people in Mogadishu, and in which he plays a role.

"I mean it. Good work, Shidde. Our people need this comedy to show issues in a different way to all the negative seriousness shown, such as the deadlocked political stalemates, tribal wars, warlords and terrorists on the T.V all the time. Hopefully, the national theatre will be refurbished and ready for shows soon." This was December 2012.

The national theatre, which was partly destroyed by suicide bombings and militia wars, has now been fully refurbished in 2020-07-21.

Lunch finished, Mr Solution was walking towards the hotel, passing the statehouse, when he noticed all these big boards advertising education courses from various universities and schools, all in Mogadishu.

Since the fall of the socialist military regime in 1991, there had been a complete stop to or decline of all government institutions that used to provide public services such as education, health, communication, transport etc., which resulted in the unqualified, under-resourced, opportunistic, money-motivated private sector filling the gap unregulated.

The following week, Mr Solution visited some of the many so-called universities and schools which operated in the city. Mr Solution noticed the focus of teachers and business owners was on quantity of fee-paying students, not on quality of education given.

Mr Solution met some of the young university students in a coffee shop near the hotel as they had just come out of the building next door which ad an advertising board in front saying they were a university. This was early 2013.

The students were sitting down drinking tea, complaining about the fees to study and the lack of qualified teachers. "Salaam xooga iyo maskaxda dalka," said Mr Solution, meaning "peace to you, the strength and brains of the country".

"Peace to you, Mister," said the students.

"I hope you don't mind; I heard your conversations. Can I ask, do you have a student union which you are all members of so they can address your concerns to the relevant people?"

"No, Mister, we did not know about this."

"Well, I heard somewhere before that wrong or poor-quality education can destroy a country quicker than a bullet. Meet me here tomorrow and I will create a student union charter in the Somali national language and hopefully, you students can meet together and form a student union for all the university students, as this appears very wrong to me."

The following day, a student union charter was downloaded and translated by Mr Solution on his laptop, then saved to a USB, from which prints were made at this internet shop near the hotel. The translated printed papers were delivered to the students that evening. "Here it is, the student union charter on how to form a student union; its beneficial to you all. Good luck, fight back by knowing your rights, and with unity, you can change what is wrong with the education system. Remember, with this union, you aren't just complaining anymore; you guys will have a tool allowing you to do something about it".

Back at the hotel, Mr Solution was meeting new and old MPs, presidential candidates, making recommendations for them to use as a campaigning policy for the education sector in the country, particularly this city, how it needed urgent reform and suggesting these so-called universities needed to be consolidated to around 4 only, as a city this size did not need around 15 to 20 universities backed with government regulations and monitoring.

"The truth is, they are like shops selling anything without checks or control, not education places. Also, the terrorist groups we are fighting have many schools as there is no law enforcement agency cracking down on them," said Mr Solution.

Heads nodded but they were unsure how to make changes. One suggested drafting education laws in parliament, but Mr Solution suggested research should be conducted by the government of all former public schools now under the management of private individuals, to find out what the teaching syllabus was, and how many students and teachers there were in them first, then allocate funds to the education ministry at once to renationalise them under direct control of the federal government.

All of us sitting and discussing this were in a complete agreement that urgent intervention must happen as the youth of today were critically important to defending and rebuilding the country. However, one presidential candidate, who owns several private schools that have used national facilities for the past 20 plus years, had no intentions to return it for public use although he is running for the highest office in the country; the presidency.

The meeting is finished with the agreement each one of us engages and plants seeds of changes in this sector individually and collectively.

The following week was spent mostly writing the Peace Cup proposal on the hotel roof and in the room. The Independent Service Cooperative is an organisation created by Mr Solution to organise and manage the project.

The main purpose of the Peace Cup was to get funding to build and refurbish sporting stadiums, then organise a football competition where teams from all 18 provinces of Somalia could compete, the aim being that it would bolster the unity of the country politically and socially while using sports to build the peace.

It also aimed to create green public areas such as parks for children and families to meet, play and rest. The aim of this was that the security in these areas would improve while a positive image of the capital would emerge, replacing the broken, bombed, bullet-holed buildings all over the city.

Since funding was becoming hard to attract for the Peace Cup proposal, Mr Solution changed his approach by contacting some civil servants such as directors-general of certain departments like the sports and culture department, who, frankly, are clueless individuals. So, the written plan was shown to them and also emailed to them directly, hoping they would take the proposal to minsters, NGOs, FIFA and friendly governments such as Turkey, to make it a reality.

Today, the peace garden or beerta nabada, as known in the Somali language, has been created by Turkish agencies, Banadir local authority, in a 2.5-kilometre square area. Previously, it was a motor vehicle scrapyard and dumping ground for the city's waste as the cities cleaning and environmental authority was not functioning due to the malfunction of the Somali authority previously.

It is also located right in the middle of the city opposite the statehouse. Terrorist groups and criminals used to hide deadly weapons and bombs used to attack civilians and government institutions there before it was developed. Today it's a green beautiful place where children and families play and relax showing a different picture emerging from the capital.

Stadium Konis, formerly a basketball stadium, has been built fully functional, partly funded by FIFA and turned into a football stadium hosting several major football competitions, including the one intended originally of the Somali regions playing each other. Puntland region was the winner in 2016 with their goalkeeper, sent from Togdheer region, whose family just happened to be neighbours of Mr Solution in Burao City, Northern Somalia.

The favourite restaurant of Mr Solution, as well as most visitors to Mogadishu, The Village restaurant, is always busy with people coming to eat, have meetings, socialise with friends or smoke the fruity-flavoured hookah pipe, or shiisha as it's known in Somalia, in the back garden. This is usually popular with ladies for some reason. Mr Solution was there most days for lunch or dinner and on this day, while chilling with a friend nicknamed the Daone, he met these reporters from the UK who were making a documentary called Dispatches, about the chefs of Mogadishu or something similar, with Aiden Hartley and, after a brief chat, participated in it with a short interview to discuss the work of Chef Mo.

Mr Solution did his little bit on it, contacts were exchanged with Aiden, who Mr Solution kept calling Adrian by mistake, who tells him about a book he wrote called the Zanzibar Chest and how he is a fellow African living in Kenya now but was born in Northern Somalia, in a place called Hargeisa. The cameraman was a Londoner like Mr Solution.

Opposite the hotel, in a big 3-floor apartment block, is the home of a pretty young lady whose father is a retired former Somali navy admiral. One day, while sitting outside the hotel with a few other guys, commenting on the attractiveness of the young girl, Mr Solution said, "I would like to meet her father to discuss how the nation can rebuild its navy to police our long seas and what role he can play in the process." One of the guy's said, "Sure; when he comes home tomorrow evening, I will call you".

Mr Solution wrote a 1-page document on his laptop and printed it out with a plan for the retired admiral to teach in the old navy school with fresh young men in the new Somali navy, or equip and train the so-called Somali pirates as official Somali navy personnel since they had knowledge of the sea already.

Mr Solution gave the document to a man who said he knew the admiral well and would deliver it to him personally. It included a business card of the people's party of Somalia, with information and a mobile contact number written on the back.

Mr Solution had made a point of visiting the camps of the displaced people around the city since first arriving in Mogadishu and, while distributing small amounts of money to each household for them to use for basic requirements such as food and water, he met a mother who had just given birth to a daughter named Miriam. Every other month, or on special occasions such as Eid, visits were made to the displaced camps to give bags of sweets and snacks to the children, in addition to some bundles of Somali currency to families, particularly the mother of Miriam who had travelled from her farm 300 kilometres away on foot due to the war between Somali military forces fighting the terrorist group Al-Shabaab, who captured the province without any obstacles previously.

Baby Miriam and her mother were doing well. A wedding party was being held on this day for two young couples from the Somali Bantu tribes, with drums being played and dancing. Mr Solution went over and joined the wedding celebration and noticed the wedding ceremony and dancing style was different from the ones usually accustomed to in the northern provinces of Somalia but extremely fun.

One of the guests, named Siido, said to Mr Solution, while sitting drinking qahwa, a Somali-style coffee with ginger, and eating grilled corn, "The couple are from Middle Shabelle province. Their tribe is called the shiidle tribe. They are very nice people, generally farmers, who grow lots of food for the country but need stability and resources to farm better. Also, you can see all those tall beautiful women shaking their booty are in abundance there; I think you would like it should you visit." Mr

Solution was sweating from dancing with the wedding party in a circle inside the IDP camp.

Mr Solution said, "Yes, thanks, I will hopefully visit soon; I have already been planning on getting out of Mogadishu to see the neighbouring provinces for some time now."

A week after this, Mr Solution travelled to Jowhar, Middle Shabelle. The road was rough or non-existent as years of no maintenance had taken its toll. The journey ended in a place called Bal'ad town, due to security information received by the national NGO, who were travelling there to promote agricultural activities, as food security is a priority in the country.

A day and night were spent in villages with a farming community to train them, give some farming equipment and also to give morale-boosting speeches.

Mr Solution met this nice family who owned a small farm with these mud houses, who insisted Mr Solution stayed the with them in their house while the NGO team stayed for the night in a little guest house nearby.

Tasty local food made with local ingredients such as mangos and chillies was made for dinner. It was getting dark as there either were no electric lamps, or torches were used mainly. A tall, slim, very dark lady served the food to Mr Solution with a pretty smile.

After dinner, the cheeky girl took Mr Solution for a walk inside the farm full of maize for an unexpected but nice evening, then sneaked back into the mud hut house for some sleep before the early morning travel back to Mogadishu took place.

The next day, early in the morning, just before leaving, there was heavy fighting between the Somali army and a terrorist group found in the area. Mr Solution was very concerned as direct gunfire was coming into the mud hut he had been staying in for the night, so, he decided to get out, running through the farm, only carrying a hand pistol, shooting back at odd times as there were men shooting at him. Then finally, he found the main road towards Mogadishu, where two pickup trucks (known as abdi bille's) belonging to Somali forces were luckily there. What a relief! They had also been in a firefight with the terrorists. Mr Solution knew personally one of the generals leading the fight against the Al-Shabaab terrorist group and recognised one of the young soldiers seen before while chatting with the general in Mogadishu. He told his military leader, "He is one of the good guys. I know him; let him on board," so he quickly boarded the truck, dripping with sweat from all the running, sitting on the edge with legs out like soldiers, back to Mogadishu.

Next month saw him meeting security officials, some diplomats from various countries rebuilding their embassies in the capital after been away for a long time, and foreign NGO organisations working in Somalia who were receiving millions if not billions of dollars in foreign aid. However, Mr Solution saw that less than 20% of the funds donated to these NGOs actually did anything tangible or physically went into the country to improve the lives of ordinary people, as he had visited where the needs were greatest, or hard to reach locations, inaccessible to these organisations for security reasons.

A dinner was organised between Mr Solution and some officials from the UNPOS, private company's employees, some journalists and academics doing research. After a lavish 3-course meal, Mr Solution got a call. It was his driver, who had been told to come and collect him around 10:30 pm to take him to the hotel.

Just before leaving, he said, "Thanks for a lovely evening. Please, don't take it as being ungrateful, but this is evidence that of all the funds being claimed to be donated to help Somalia in aid, 90% of the time it is spent on flights, hotels, bogus report-writing, and unnecessary seminars, mainly outside of Somalia. As I was saying earlier, if only 70% was directly invested into the country and 30% was used for great parties and dinners, the speed of change would be like nothing seen before."

Mr Solution knew this would upset some of them as they had got used to being unopposed or challenged over having a jolly great time on the back of showing needy people, but his conscience told him to tell it to them straight. Who cares if they don't invite you to these nice dinner parties anymore? It's your people you are fighting for and they come first; after all, you are the leader of the people's party of Somalia.

Seeing all these unused or partly destroyed buildings all over the city had attracted the attention of Mr Solution, who decided to set up a real estate business to refurbish, rebuild, manage, rent or sell them to citizens inside the country and abroad.

Creating this would be easy as Mr Solution used to own a company abroad dealing in real estate, or an estate agency as it's called in the UK, so the logo of his former company was redesigned with a new company name.

The formation and registration were done quickly. Mr Solution decided to give a 50% share partnership to a young Mogadishu resident studying at university who also owned a small office providing internet and printing services inside a hotel room.

The reason for this generous stake in the business was because this new partner had knowledge of the housing market, and the city's residents, while Mr Solution had the business experience and some funding to rent and resource an office.

Office furniture was purchased a few days later from the biggest market in East Africa, Bakara market, and shop sign posters were printed ready to display.

A few days later, while sitting outside a coffee shop with some people, discussing how the political process was going and how best to shape it to make it work best under the circumstances, Mr Solution saw 2 gentlemen walking past, firstly on his side of the road, then crossing to the opposite side,   then returning. Mr Solution recognised one who used to live in London, working in a Somali-owned money remittance business from northern Somalia. The other was also from London and was a travel agent, later becoming a minster in the self-declared Somaliland region in northern Somalia.

As suspected by their unusual behaviour, previous knowledge of the individuals abroad and political interests, it was confirmed that they were here to be problematic to Mr Solution and the Somali government's election process.

Mr Solution waved and called one of the men over, shaking his hand. "Long time, no see. I was not expecting to meet you here in the capital; how long are you staying and what are you doing here?' He replied, "We are here on a business trip; this is Mr Kadare, also from the UK".

Shortly after, we parted company, but not before we exchanged contact numbers. A few days later, Mr Solution, had a meeting with a real estate developer in Mogadishu who builds large buildings for commercial and diplomatic purposes, such as renting to embassies, as there is a very profitable return on the monthly rental income.

This real estate developer was a man Mr Solution knew personally and he hoped a partnership could be made between his newly created company and the real estate developer to manage his large property portfolio. As the car driving Mr Solution approached the house of the real estate developer, a small car was leaving, being driven by the two men Mr Solution had met a few days earlier, who were spies. "Stop the car! Here is your money. Drop me here and follow that car to its destination. Once they stop, call me too".

Entering the house, Mr Solution was told to wait in a large courtyard inside the house by a maid who said she would inform her boss that the scheduled meeting with Mr Solution was now and that he had arrived. "What would you like to drink?" "A cold watermelon juice please," he said. The drinks and an ashtray arrived.

After waiting for about 20 minutes, the maid returned and said, "Unfortunately, the house owner is away on a business trip. Can I take a message"? 'Strange one,' he thought, but he continued, "Yes, you can take this envelope. It has all the documents for our proposal. Please hand it to him ASAP".

The taxi driver called as Mr Solution was walking down the road to catch a taxi to a restaurant for lunch. "Where are you, my friend? I need a taxi from this hot sun." He said, "I am outside your hotel as the car you asked me to follow has stopped there to meet and pick up the super heavy ladies." Mr Solution said, "Good work, my friend, thanks." They are called super heavy ladies because of their physical size being very large.

Back at the hotel after lunch, Mr Solution found an invitation card pushed under his hotel room door. It read, "You are kindly invited to a wedding, Mr Solution." This was done by the bride, also from Europe, staying in the room opposite, who was marrying a young tribal chief in Mogadishu to select his clan's member of parliament.

The rooms opposite Mr Solution had been booked by the bride-to-be, her friends, relatives and a Somali singer who had been called over from Nairobi, Kenya to perform at the wedding.

A night of chewing the potent khat stimulant and partying was planned as the wedding started at 8 pm and was scheduled to finish around midnight. These other girls from the central provinces of Somalia, also visiting Mogadishu on a mission of some kind, invited Mr Solution to join their party in their room before the wedding, and the invitation was graciously accepted.

One of the girls said she had run away from her former crazy husband who was the son of some former president of that regional government in Somalia; she also said he was the broker of the Somali pirates in the region with millions of dollars.

Mr Solution noticed all her luggage was by Louis Vuitton and bundles of cash in dollars were removed in

$100 bills to order drinks and more khat to be delivered by hotel employees.

The money was cash taken from her former husband who was the pirate's boss or broker. This was quite clear to Mr Solution, but he did not object to this curvy lady spending it on him or the party, but was not comfortable with getting involved romantically with her, due to her background, although lots of flirting and play-fighting was done in the qaaci sitting session.

An afternoon of chewing khat, with intense conversations from hot ladies in bras and silky blouses, with perfumes often being sprayed and incense being burned was enjoyed until 9:30 pm, when Mr Solution left, in his tailor-made suit from London, to go to another hotel where the wedding party was being held.

The wedding party was warming up nicely, with plenty of guests and live music being played,

It was a hot humid night, made even hotter for Mr Solution by all the chewing of khat, and smoking before. "Waiter, can I get a cold bottle of water, please? I will be sitting outside here in the courtyard." The waiter did not return, so Mr Solution went on a walkabout searching for water around the hotel and, along the way, found these Turkish workmen who were hotel residents and invited them to the wedding party. Lots of dancing was done, Somali-style, by the Turkish men who told me they enjoyed the wedding party.

A few days later, after living in the hotel for around 6 months, Mr Solution met this man who was a former Somali MP in the transitional previous government. He had been born in Mogadishu, however, his clan from his father's side originated from northern Somalia, regionally administered by Somaliland authorities as part of the new Somali federal system in place over the last 10 to 15 years. He lived in a shared house with another man whose wife recently gave birth. He occupied two rooms in this place with his third wife, but with no children.

After meeting several times afterwards in the hotel lobby, he suggested to Mr Solution to come and move into the empty room in his place. "I will think about it, thanks," said Mr Solution. What was there to think about?

"Where is your hotel room? It's a safe quiet area directly opposite this hotel, next door to the police station. "You don't have to pay any money and fresh food is cooked daily." Quickly he ran upstairs, gathered the luggage, collected the pistol he carried everywhere from the reception and said, "This man is checking out."

Mr Solution was not sure about this erratic gun-waving, toothless man's offer of accommodation, however, thought he might be useful in order to accomplish a few things as he was a local man who had knowledge of political and security matters in Mogadishu.

Mr Solution checked out of the hotel but left some important documents and some money in the hotel safe. On the first night in his small shared accommodation with him and his wife chewing the potent khat stimulant and discussing many different things, he mentioned how he was fighting to get his stolen parliamentary seat back in this new administration via the Somali judiciary, justly or with his gun.

Tours of his birth house, the district he was raised in and meeting of his married sisters were done. One of his sisters was married to a wealthy businessman who owned a hotel and she now was the MP in the new Somali parliament.

He felt the wealthy businessman from a different tribe had robbed him of his seat by using his sister, who was the man's wife, as a parliamentary so he could get his clansman elected as president of Somalia. This made sense as the national parliament elects the president who then appoints a prime minister to form a government.

The parliament is formed using a tribal dynamics system called 4.5, with a 30% quota set aside for women. This was a policy created by Mr Solution while in the UK and finally being implemented while in Mogadishu. When he had a meeting with politicians and tribal leaders, he asked them, "Do you have a mother, sister, wife or daughter who are all women?" and when they all answered yes, he recommended they elect women to parliament by allowing a proposed compulsory quota to be made for them, which they reluctantly agreed to as this was difficult for African men generally.

Shabeel (meaning tiger), his Somali nickname, was furiously complaining about why women were being given a compulsory 30% stake and how his tribal chief had been corruptly bought to select someone else.

Mr Solution was hot after all the khat-chewing and was explaining that it was the normal democratic process being exercised allowing women their right to be legislators, which was good for the country, but working hard to make sure he did not become aware of the fact it was Mr Solution's idea to elect women to parliament, just in case he pulled his pistol up and pointed it at Mr Solution as this man was very erratic and unpredictable, to say the least, and took the pistol everywhere, even to the toilet.

Many days were spent doing interviews, participating in debates on the phone to local radio stations such as Dalsan, and Mogadishu city radio, Shabelle mainly and, on occasions, with the VOA Somali service about current affairs in Somalia and the region.

A month later, Mr Solution moved out of the dodgy former MP's house and into a rented single room with a shared toilet recommended by a young guy who approached Mr Solution saying he had a room available next to the house where he lived. He was from

Mogadishu. This happened while having lunch alone in a restaurant in the middle of town, as he overheard a conversation regarding a place to rent.

Mr Solution said, "Ok, I would like to view it today if possible." A viewing was arranged quickly as the person who owned the place was a relative of this young man. Upon visiting the place, Mr Solution noticed it was a very built-up area with lots of small houses very close to each other, with a tall water tank from a borehole powered by a loud generator.

The property was a single unfurnished room next to another room lived in by a single mother with a three-year-old daughter. Mr Solution said, "Hey, thanks, but I think I will leave it." The young man said, "But Mister, it's cheap, there are no water charges as the water is supplied by the tank next door owned by my uncle and family, it's a safe area as all the surrounding people are my clan members who will look after you like their own and I live in the empty house next door where you can chill out with me".

"It's unfurnished, man. I was hoping to find a furnished place, buddy."

"We can go to the market now and buy what you need to make the room work for you, it's no trouble."

Mr Solution was reluctant but said, "Ok, let's go to the market." A small bed, a fan cooler, a little carpet, a clothes hanger and a table were purchased and delivered to the room by donkey that day.

Mr Solution, who was very adaptable to most environments if need be, was settling into his new neighbourhood and getting to know the local people. The owner of the water rig selling water to the neighbourhood was a man aged around 60, from Mogadishu. He was married to a current Somali female MP, originally from northern Somalia now administered by the self-declared independent Somaliland region but officially and legally part of Somalia.

Mr Solution was introduced to the lady MP by the husband one day. She said, "I am from Hargeisa and you?" Mr Solution replied, "I am also from northern Somalia but Burao, Togdheer province." Mr Solution noticed she had a set of gold teeth which was clipped to either side of the front ones.

Mr Solution was thinking it was not a coincidence that the previous former MP and this current lady MP were both from the north of the country. It also became apparent that the lady MP could read or write but was making up the numbers for the new parliament as it was based on regional or tribal association. He thought it was strange, to say the least, but moved on from it.

A month later, a man, who was a relative of the lady MP, came to stay in a room in the house next door, lived in by the guy who rented this room out. Also, one night, while sitting outside the door, he approached Mr Solution, introducing himself as a top chef from Hargeisa looking for work in Mogadishu who was also the cousin of the MP next door by clan affiliation. He said he had been promised a job in a hotel by its owner, who was still doing some construction work on it, so in the meantime, he was paid 10 dollars a day pocket money until the building was completed and he could start work.

He did not ask what Mr Solution did or what he was doing in Mogadishu, but he acted like he knew about Mr Solution by his clan. Mr Solution noticed how this man followed him around, turning up sometimes dressed exactly like him when having meetings with people, interrupting and being rude. A few nights later, sitting outside the rented room, the same man approached saying that when he was a taxi driver in Hargeisa, he used to do this and that.

Mr Solution said, "I thought you were a chef over there." He said, "Yes, I was and I just got a new job as a cook in a restaurant in Lido beach and start tomorrow." 'He is telling lie after lie,' thought Mr Solution, changing his story all the time, but he said, "Well done, man, all the best." A few days later, the restaurant he said he was employed in got blown up apparently by a bomb placed under a car, causing many casualties.

One evening, as he sat outside on a concrete couch chatting to a neighbour, Mr Solution, who had been suspicious of this guy's stories and intentions, was visited by him, along with another man who was very loud and smelling of onions.

Mr Solution realised they had been drinking a lot of gin as a bottle almost fell down to the ground from them. They had been drinking elsewhere and using the onions to disguise the smell of it, as drinking alcohol was considered forbidden and illegal by law in the country recently, although it was imported in large quantities from neighbouring countries.

Some hours later, a text message was received by Mr Solution from the man who had gone inside to continue his drinking next door. It read "You cannot do anything to Somaliland and you will fail with your political activities in Mogadishu as we will not allow it; we will block and discredit you".

Mr Solution replied "I think you're confused, misinformed, paranoid and will become very dizzy eventually, when all is said and done. Also, you should not send threatening messages to people you do not know much about".

One day, while chilling in a coffee shop nearby, Mr Solution showed the message to the young guy whose house it was, advising him to be careful with him. He also got a local guy who worked for the Somali security service to monitor him, as he could have been the person behind the deadly bombings in the city recently.

The single mother living in the room next door seemed to be very careless with her child's wellbeing as the kid did not use the toilet, but rather shit or urinated outside the property often. Also, Mr Solution felt uncomfortable with seeing the young mother's half-naked body in bed with the door wide open when he entered the shared flat, so he decided to move out as soon as possible and started to look for another place.

One day Mr Solution was walking down the main road of the city towards where the foreign office was located and the newly created business office which Mr Solution set up. This route was a common one that Mr Solution took most days when going to this office but, on this day, he just briefly stopped at a little tin-roofed shop to buy something, when a huge loud bomb explosion happened by a busy roundabout maybe 100 yards away from where he was standing. Dark smoke filled the air, with flying debris everywhere.

Shocked, Mr Solution looked around. There were dead body parts, burning buildings and cars. There was the burning body of a man disabled from the waist down, who used to beg sitting on the side of the road. Mr Solution used to give him bundles of money most mornings. Shocked by this, Mr Solution attempted to put the fire out on the dead man but had no water, so stamped on him with his feet, then stopped as the person was already dead. Human body parts were visible all around.

Mr Solution checked his arms and feet. He thought, "Thank God it's all there," and calmly walked past the scene to take shelter in a hotel near

where the small office, recently set up for the real estate business, was located. Sporadic gunfire was heard coming from the Somali military and police attempting to cordon the area off from people while some kind of order and clear up was done.

The private security guards of the hotel, who were heavily armed with AK47s, instructed Mr Solution not to return outside to view the mess after the bombing, as stray bullets could easily hit someone, so Mr Solution calmly walked into the hotel restaurant and ordered a glass of fresh grapefruit juice.

After the last residency, Mr Solution found and moved into a new place within a house accommodating a family, next door to one of the city's district offices, with a basketball court inside it's compound as it was a safe neighbourhood within easy reach of most places in the city.

The room had its own side door entrance, it was clean, had running water and the rent was 50 dollars per month. The mother of the house was a veteran nurse who ran the local mother and child health centre within the district offices compound. She had a newly married son and two daughters, one with children, living in the 4-bedroom house.

The son was a singer with a group from the city, who wrote and recorded songs for the capital's provincial council and the national T.V stations, to communicate an awareness of the importance of peace, development, and unity. Some days, the son and group founder were in the house discussing material.

The middle daughter had 2 young sons. Her husband lived in a Middle Eastern country for work purposes. The youngest daughter was aged 17 or 18 years old and studied in a school. To the surprise of Mr Solution, he recognised the young daughter from some months earlier when she was playing handball in the local sports centre when he visited to shoot some hoops with some lads.

Mr Solution recalled she was being trained by a young man who was man-handling her in an inappropriate manner and Mr Solution intercepted and said, "Stop the way you are handling her! Don't forget she is a Somali girl and we don't touch them like that. This should be the way to demonstrate defensive posture".

The people stopped and noticed this as he showed care and genuine concern for the dignity and respect of the girl. Towards the end, as Mr Solution was leaving the basketball court, he passed the young lady sitting courtside and said, "You are very athletic, young lady," and she said with a smile, "Can you handle this, old man?" clearly showing her curvy athletic body shape. Mr Solution smiled, looked back then continued walking off.

Mr Solution did not mention to the youngest daughter that he remembered her, but introduced himself as the new tenant renting the available room. Somehow, though, it was no coincidence that he had been recommended to rent this room by a young man from Kismayo without some kind of plan.

Mr Solution was spending time with the son of the household and the founder of his band named Deegan, who was also a writer and performer, showing them the website of the XSS party and social media pages with lots of content they may be able to use in the lyrics of their songs to broaden their messages. This was done deliberately by Mr Solution to raise certain issues which must be dealt with head-on by all, and shape other matters.

Some weeks later, Mr Solution went to a district called Afgooye, 30 kilometres outside of Mogadishu, to see and work with an NGO who worked with young people recruited as child soldiers by terrorist groups. Their aim was to reverse the wrongful radicalisation of these children by terror groups by providing education, training, and tools for employment while providing food rations to their families.

Mr Solution spent the day registering and talking to the young people on how they could have a bright future and became good young citizens by taking the necessary steps and opportunities in front of them provided by this organisation.

A four-day training seminar, organised for national NGOs working in the capital, was held near the airport in a well-known hotel called the Peace Hotel by UN-funded organisations. Mr Solution had been asked to be an interpreter for the sessions, as he is trilingual. This was done independently. Once the 4-day session was finished, somebody from a UN agency asked Mr Solution if he would like a job working for them. Mr Solution said, "Thanks for the offer. Can you please give me your card and contact details? I shall contact you with a reply".

Although the people he worked with during the four days were interesting people from various countries around the world, he felt the job's salary was not that attractive. It would also distract him from his political aspirations and the work he had been doing independently and successfully for his country and people.

A meeting was scheduled with a very inspiring pretty young Somali girl, who returned to Mogadishu from abroad to help her people and country and who is the director of an NGO about peace and human rights. Regretfully, however, Mr Solution had to cancel as he had plans to travel to a coastal city called Marka the following day.

This province had, for a long time, been a stronghold of the terrorist group Al-Shabaab. Large parts, including the rich fertile agricultural districts which used to grow much of the country's food, were still controlled by the group.

Marka, being the province's capital, had been cleared and taken back by Somali forces supported by African Union soldiers. At that time, it was 90 kilometres away from the Somali capital by road.

Mr Solution consulted a trusted Somali military soldier about the trip whose commanding general was the man leading the liberation of Mogadishu from the terrorist group also involved in the recapture of Marka, recently nicknamed "dhegabadan". Unfortunately, this general was killed in a terrorist attack on the Mogadishu Saxaafi Hotel he had lived in for some years. The terrorist group stormed the hotel, but the general went down fighting.

One of his young soldiers said the roads were rough, attacks from IEDs and gunfights were common along the way, so he advised him to take at least 2 well-equipped pickup trucks full of soldiers.

Mr Solution said thanks and rode off with the soldiers on their pickup truck to a little restaurant known for its meat dishes. "Stop the car" said Mr Solution. He entered the restaurant, where a huge pot of food had been cooked at the back on a wood fire. He asked the person at the counter, "Is the lamb ready?"

"Yes, it's ready, and the rice too."

"Good; how much is the whole lamb pot and all the rice of the day?" It was more than 100 dollars, so he said, "Ok, include the pots in the cost as well. Here is 150 dollars. Load it all on the back of those soldiers' trucks and thanks again".

Food loaded up, Mr Solution told the soldiers to drive directly to their barracks and enjoy the food, to keep up the good work but he would be fine and did not need a military escort to Marka.

Mr Solution knew the community dynamics that lived in the province and felt taking heavily armed soldiers would draw lots of attention which could be more dangerous than if he went alone or with just 1 or 2 others.

Mr Solution called his usual taxi driver, Sanju, whose car had been locked by the traffic police in their compound. Mr Solution knew this man's clan connections to the biggest tribe that lived in the province. Also, his father was a tribal chief in another province.

Mr Solution said, "Sanju, would you like to get a break from Mogadishu and come with me to Marka for a few days? I will cover all expenses." Sanju replied, "I would love to; the city has been depressing me lately."

"Ok, good. Pack a little bag and I will see you tomorrow morning at 8 am. We have to catch a minibus.

A phone call was made to a local respected man from the majority tribe in the province, who lived in Marka and was related to the family Mr Solution was staying with in Mogadishu, to inform him of the visit scheduled for tomorrow and for him to book a hotel room with 2 beds.

Sanju was collected from his house inside an IDP camp. Sanju showed him a tunnel, dug up by the terrorist group while they were controlling fighting in Mogadishu, covered up by a carpet inside the bedroom he lived in. Mr Solution was a little concerned but said, "Come, let's go. We have to catch our bus from the Bakara market." The bus was already loading up people with their shopping stuff. They visited the khat dealer and purchased some, as it would make the journey pass quicker and be more interesting. Usually, the bus was packed full with ordinary citizens who came to Mogadishu for shopping, trading goods and visiting families now returning to their homes outside.

The views along the way were beautiful and green, with lots of farming land, but the road between the cities was completely destroyed, needing urgent repair which would improve the ability of farmers to bring their produce to markets in the capital in time for domestic consumption and export.

Along the way, there were checkpoints manned by unofficial men dressed in military uniforms, all extorting money illegally from the driver of the bus and towards the end of the journey, approaching our destination, the driver purposely failed to stop, continuing behind a convoy of African Union military trucks as he did not want to pay monies demanded by the illegal checkpoints anymore. However, the goons quickly raised their AK47s, firing some shots. Mr Solution immediately told the driver to stop the bus as he could get himself killed, along with the passengers he was responsible for, which included lots of women and children.

The minibus stopped and the driver got out to discover that the men of the illegal checkpoint were very angry with his actions. One of the goons said, "Do you think you can get away and the African Union aliens will protect you? We are the authorities of our province and you will pay!" Arguments followed and one of the goons pointed his gun at the driver's chest then, slapping him across the face, said, "You are a dead man." Quickly, Mr Solution jumped out of the minibus, although passengers and Sanju were telling him not to, but he ignored their concerns and went to mediate and calm the dangerous situation.

Mr Solution told the driver to apologise to the goons and the goons to understand this man was fed up as all the profits he made had been taken by the last 3 checkpoints that were very greedy and, because of these unreasonable guys, he was thinking of stopping this treacherous journey he made daily to transport the public and earn a living to support his family. He then said, "I am telling you this as I am a Somali citizen from northern Somalia, as you can tell by my accent."

The goon smiled and asked what his tribe was? Mr Solution replied, also telling him to point his gun away from his direction. He said to the bus driver, "You are lucky today as this man was with you. You can go, but next time, try this stunt again and you will taste these bullets from my gun."

The journey continued to Marka, arriving around 4 pm. On entering the city, via the only viable road, on the left-hand side, Mr Solution noticed a white two-storey building with Togdheer Hotel on it, directly facing the beach of the Indian Ocean. "Stop, driver, this is my stop!" The bags, large quantities of khat and Sanju got off and approached the hotel's front door. There was a little shop next door. A young man left his chair and entered the building. "Do you have rooms available?" asked Mr Solution.

"Yes, we do."

"Two single rooms, please."

The hotel was quite basic, but they were happy they had made it without much trouble.

Mr Solution phoned his contact in Marka, informing him they had arrived and booked in to the Togdheer Hotel at the end of the city. "Good," he said," I am coming to see you now." They met the man named Yusuf, a very nice man, and he said he only lived a few roads behind us and this area was a safe area as all the people living around here were part of the clan who would look after them if they needed it.

Drinks and some essentials were purchased from the shop next door; Mr Solution said, "Keep the change and put it towards the donations for the town's hospital."

The rest of the evening was spent chewing the khat they had brought, and watching the beautiful views of the ocean from the rooftop and all the neighbouring white buildings in the town.

"Sanju, at 6 am we are going for a swim in the sea opposite. Go and tell the hotel guy downstairs to let us out in the morning".

They had an early morning swim in the cool Indian Ocean, with some pictures taken showing the beauty of it, and then they met Yusuf to go into the town for breakfast and to explore the town and the people.

Mr Solution noticed this town had many unique-looking mosques and old classical buildings, the people were warm and welcoming but had suffered under the control of the terrorist group who controlled the seaside town. There was also a lack of services from the Somali government such as security, health and education.

The town's hospital was closed and not functioning at all when they visited, although, it had a decent building which only needed human resources to make it work.

Mr Solution and Sanju visited the town hall where the newly appointed governor was with few of his soldiers. After a brief meeting, Mr Solution promised, upon his return to Mogadishu, to highlight the plight of the people with the new Somali government and international organisations who could help.

He received a phone call from a close family member from his home town of Burao, Togdheer, saying she was at Berbera waiting for a plane to come to Mogadishu tomorrow. Mr Solution attempted to convince her to stay there, as he would come over there when he was done with his work here, but she refused, so, after two days in Marka, a return trip to Mogadishu was planned. Also returning to Mogadishu was a man who came to see his wife and kids. He was married to the daughter of the lady Mr Solution had rented the room from in Mogadishu.

After another day in the seaside town, the minibus journey to Mogadishu was booked and, late in the evening, they arrived back safely at the house. The next day, pictures of Mr Solution's trip, swimming on Marka beach with some local people, were posted on social media. Many people were surprised at these pictures as most people, including the Somali government officials, were afraid to travel there due to Al-Shabaab terror group operating in that region, one post read, "Surprised to see you there as that town and region belongs to Al-Shabaab." Mr Solution's response was, "Marka belongs to the good people of Marka, not Al-Shabaab as you say. It's been liberated; did you not know?"

A very wealthy Somali businessman, who was proud of the quiet but effective work Mr Solution was doing in the country, said, "I will fund your campaign fully to be the next president if you put your name down as a candidate." Mr Solution agreed, but as many opportunistic candidates, including the incoming president, were afraid of this mysterious young Mr Solution, they put a condition down that the age of the presidential candidate must be 40 or above, meaning Mr Solution, who was 36 at the time, would not meet the criteria to run.

Mr Solution gave some feedback about the trip to Marka to some government officials from the defence department and parliamentary members who were supposed to represent the lower Shabelle province but had not visited or been aware of the real situation on the ground there. Mr Solution explained about the clan wars which had been problematic there, the non-functioning hospital of the province due to lack of resources, and the frequent raids by the terror group who still controlled important districts of the province, particularly the agricultural districts like Janaale.

"I recommend that you, as the people's representatives, visit and do your jobs," said Mr Solution, and he left the meeting in protest. Some months later, the new president at the time, Hassan Sheik, and some of his ministers, including the defence minister named Fiqi, took a helicopter ride to Marka provided by the UN, doing exactly what Mr Solution did by swimming in the sea and posing for pictures. 'Not original, but copy cats,' thought Mr Solution.

A few days after returning to Mogadishu, Mr Solution saw the younger sister of the house he was staying in, striking seductive poses and wearing figure-hugging colourful dresses made by the highly skilled tailors trading in the city, who should really be funded to mass-produce their works. This happened all the time, especially in the mornings when Mr Solution woke up and went to use the shared bathroom, and late evenings when he returned to sleep.

Mr Solution felt shy all of a sudden, if not uncomfortable, as he lived in the same property as the rest of her family. Usually, Mr Solution would not hesitate to flirt or show some love to the young lady but, under these circumstances, decided that control and restraint must be shown, although, it was becoming difficult. Sometimes, when the house was empty of others except Mr Solution, the girl who is taunting him with her beauty. He feared this could side-track him from important matters. Also, opposing people could use it in a political move to blackmail him if he gave in to her seductions and got caught in a very compromising position.

She was deliberately making this plan difficult. On this particular day, she enters the room of Mr Solution, who had been suffering from a serious malaria infection and had been in bed for 5 days. She was wearing a see-through traditional dress that had been altered to fit her body in a very tight way, along with bright red lipstick on her lips as she walked into the room with a charcoal burner with incense used to make the house smell good. "Come in," said Mr Solution. She placed the item on a small table by the side of the bed near the window where the light was coming through, bending over in a very sexual way, revealing her beautiful body as the sunlight entered from the window. Because of this, Mr Solution's feelings had been awakened, giving him the energy to stand up although very sick. He decided to continue to sit on the chair, gripping his towel to cover his lower body due to the situation. Flashes of Mr Solution and the young daughter in a very compromising position, and the mother bursting in with a weapon and catching them in the act, were playing on Mr Solution's head. However, he remained disciplined and said, "Thanks again. Can you please close the door on the way out?"

Within that week, Mr Solution became extremely sick due to malaria bites giving him a serious fever, loss of appetite, weight and taste for a week. Initially, malaria tablets bought from abroad were being taken by Mr Solution, but they failed to give any relief. The mother of the house, who was a midwife and nurse who managed the local mother and child health centre, said, "If you can walk for 5 minutes, come and see me at the clinic later. I will check you out for malaria." "Ok, thanks Mama".

Mr Solution arrived at the clinic, A little blood sample from his thumb was taken, immediately confirming malaria as the cause of the illness, so a 7-day medicine treatment, consisting of capsules made by an Italian company, was given and Mr Solution gently walked back to the house to lay down on the bed again.

Now that Mr Solution knew the cause of the sickness, he phoned a friend who had also travelled from abroad and was living in a hotel nearby owned by a Somali family from Switzerland. He explained his illness and requested 10 litres of fresh camel milk from a young female camel who had recently given birth, as Mr Solution remembered, when younger, his grandfather used to do this if any member of the family got sick due to malaria as it would make the person's stomach run, giving them energy and they would recover quickly.

The milk order was acquired from a place outside of Mogadishu where fresh milk arrived every day. Mr

Solution collected it the following day from the hotel, drinking it straight away. It would also be the first day of his recovery, after drinking the milk in addition to the medicine.

He had been living in Mogadishu for around 10 months, when a close family relative was sent from Burao, Togdheer to ask Mr Solution to return with him to northern Somalia and leave Mogadishu. The main purpose of this was to stop the work or path Mr Solution was on. However, after a 2-week period and failing to convince Mr Solution to travel back with him, this gentleman was taken to the airport with 2 bags full of fresh fruits grown in southern Somalia, such as fresh mangos, papaya and isbandeys and waved goodbye, but that's not the end. A second close family member arrived in Mogadishu from northern Somalia. Mr Solution picked her up from the airport in a taxi and said, "I have booked you a hotel." She replied, "Cancel it. I will be staying with a family while I am here."

She gave the taxi driver the address of the place and Mr Solution recognised the area as being near where the Peace Park had been newly created with a steel fence around it at the time. Mr Solution said, "Look. That large cleared area with the gate around it used to be full of scrapped cars and rubbish 6 months ago. It's taking shape nicely; do you not think?" She replied with a rude comment, saying how she did not like this city and wanted to return ASAP with me. The taxi stopped outside the family house belonging to a 1-legged amputee who previously was a member of parliament in the transitional government. He dropped the lady off, having arranged a meeting the following day for lunch and little sightseeing. Mr Solution got the feeling she would be a very challenging lady to deal with compared to the previous person.

He arrived the following day to greet the family she was staying with, then took the old lady out for lunch, followed by some sightseeing which included the offices of Mr Solution's new business venture and the Peace Park his plan had created, hoping this would impress her a little so she would return alone without any trouble. "As you can see, I have unfinished business here and you're witnessing the progress the city is making first hand with my help, so I cannot come with you to Togdheer tomorrow but will come and visit next month."

She said, "Why are you helping them? They are enemies! Come and build your own country." Mr Solution said, "This is our country. I think you mean our province. This is the capital, so in order to fix the whole country, the head must be fixed first, then the rest of the regions will start to heal and function correctly, creating opportunities for people nationwide.

Do you know I have been liaising with international NGOs here to visit our region in northern Somalia to do development projects? For example, a Turkish government agency called Tika has already taken a ship to Berbera as requested by Mr Solution after a meeting with Turkish officials in Mogadishu and they promised to construct 2 clean water rigs in our district, Bali Barwaaqo. I have personally phoned the tribal king of my clan to assist them and make sure the local Somaliland administration does not divert or stop this much-needed water project, although I don't have much confidence in him. There are bad men over there who might wish to hold the people hostage politically and economically, when they find out it was me who was behind the water project for our province, by not allowing a precious resource like water to be sourced for the people.

Let me remind you of the Somali proverb which says "one who takes care of his own also takes care of others". As you know, I have taken care of our immediate family since I was a small child, have participated in building a school and a health centre and provided sports equipment to the district town where I was born, demonstrating charity or development at home first."

The lady started crying, hitting the ground in absolute hysterics and making a terrible scene, saying she would not leave until he came with her. Mr Solution agreed but said, "I will take you back, but remember, I will have to return 5 days later. I hope you understand and won't cause trouble when we get there".

"Fine, I promise," she said. Mr Solution prepared a little hand luggage with only a few items and left all the rest of his belongings in the rented house and some things in the previous hotel storage. Upon arriving at the airport to leave for Berbera on the short flight, Mr Solution met a short Italian man Milan while outside the terminal for a cigarette break, and they began discussing football, such as each other's football teams in Italy and work in Mogadishu. The man said he was looking for somebody to work with him on a special project he was doing in Mogadishu and Mr solution should contact him on his return.

Some officials from the Somali government at the time tried to persuade Mr Solution to stay, by cancelling the initial flight scheduled that day, meaning Mr Solution had to think about his trip further for another day while a reschedule was going on.

The flight was rescheduled for the following day and, after much hustle in the deliberately unorganised chaotic Mogadishu airport, the plane took off with Mr Solution and the lady on board.

Chapter 4.
Nudging and Shaping the North, Bottom-Up and Top-Down

The plane landed on a long runway originally built by the Soviets in the late 70s, designed for military and space aircraft landings should it enter back via the African continent. The date was May 2013, and people and luggage were being unloaded on the tarmac. It was extremely hot and humid as usual on the Red Sea coast. Mr Solution took a picture of the plane and runway using his reliable Sony mobile phone then hurried to the terminal for shade and in search of a cold bottle of water. He had his leather travel bag over his shoulder and was also carrying the luggage of the close family relative who had travelled with him.

The queue for immigration was short. The lady at the desk said, "Passport, please." Mr Solution replied, I only have a ticket as I have travelled internally from Mogadishu." Some of the passengers had come from other destinations outside of Somalia, such as Uganda or Kenya, so it was normal to ask for a passport, however, the lady said, "Please come with me. The immigration officer wants to speak with you in his office."

The close family relative, who was an elderly lady, was let through and was waiting on the other side. Mr Solution thought it strange, but said, "Ok, let's go." They approached a small office in the corner. "Come in," said the officer, "and take a seat.

You travelled from Mogadishu and are travelling to Burao I see." "Yes, that's correct, as printed on the ticket."

"Are you from Burao?" "Yes, that's my home city."

"What were you doing in Mogadishu? You are a Somalilander!" "No, I am a Somali visiting the capital and working on people's affairs."

"People's affairs? Are you not from Somaliland?" "No, I am from Somalia, as stated on my passport, driving licence and birth certificate."

"Where are these documents and what does 'people's affairs' mean?"

"I don't think that's any of your business. You are wasting my time and yours. I am not a child you can brainwash, so, if you don't mind, I am thirsty so must purchase some water then continue my journey. Are we finished here? I am the only person being asked these irrelevant inappropriate questions as I can see from everyone who arrived here, plus, you know who I am, so this game is boring. Stop it; I am not laughing."

"Yes, you can go now," said the immigration officer, so he exited the terminal with his relative and went to a small shop with a tin roof. "Two bottles of cold water, please." When the shopkeeper hands over the bottle, he sees it's a bottle of water named Saxansaxo, made and bottled in Burao, Togdheer. Mr Solution smiles with delight and surprise as the name is a familiar one, precisely because, in 2006, while in Burao on vacation for 3 months and while the business was being created, the owners wanted a name so approached Mr Solution and around 10 others, who were all in a café. Mr Solution gave this name Saxansaxo to demonstrate his Somali language ability in competition with the other people, including a 65-year-old, who said at the time, "You Somalis from the Diaspora do not speak authentic Somali language." He obviously lost that game as it's the name I gave which was chosen.

The inconvenience and delay caused was washed down with a cold bottle of Saxansaxo water, then, as there were no taxi offices at the airport, a man outside said, "Come with me. I will drive you to town where a friend of mine who makes this journey to Burao will take you, but know it will cost you 100 dollars." He replied, "Listen, Mister, drive on and we will negotiate as we are local people who know the journey prices".

The town was quite empty since most people leave Berbera and go to cooler places, as the temperature can top 50 degrees. 'If there was a well-operated and affordable energy company operating in coastal cities such as Berbera and Bosaso, people would have air-conditioning in their homes and stay,' thought Mr Solution as he looks around the empty city.

After some haggling over the price for the journey, a driver was found who would take us to Burao., some pictures were taken of the nice mountains of Shiikh while driving up on the Snake Road and down the mountains, passing these little villages by the side of the road, which appeared exactly the same as Mr Solution remembered from past journeys some years earlier. Some traders were standing on the side of the road selling oranges and guava. "Thanks, but we have mangos and papaya from Mogadishu today. Maybe next time," said Mr Solution.

He took some pictures of the roads to compare with the roads in southern Somalia which were completely destroyed due to the lack of maintenance by governments over the years while institutions were non-functioning.

The main reason for the condition of the roads in the south compared to the north was because of the terrain or land composition. In the south, the soil is soft and ideal for agriculture and the north is full of mountains providing rocks and other materials, so the road is harder to break up. Also, more concrete was used as these raw materials were in abundance locally, including the national cement producer, which was based in Berbera at the time.

Tribal wars or militias, corruption and disputes were rife in northern Somalia or the Somaliland region at the time. Mr Solution had an idea how best to use the pictures of the roads by posting them on social media, saying how well the regional administration of Somaliland's road agency maintained and built the roads here. He also sent an email of it to a civil servant of that administration to get them to create a road agency which could build roads and carry out maintenance of existing roads.

The aim of this was to direct the people and the region's administration towards developments and away from the tribal wars and lessen the wasted resources on corrupt activities. This idea worked, and, to Mr Solution's surprise, a few months later, the Somaliland road agency was formed and an ambitious plan was announced to build a road from Burao Erigavo, Sanaag province, stretching for 360 kilometres.

People were talking about this ambitious road being built, and how it would create jobs and shorten the long dangerous journey currently endured by people.

Currently, in 2020, almost 180 kilometres is complete and the work is still continuing. The funds to build this road had been collected from various citizens in northern Somalia, including schoolchildren who donated their lunch monies. Citizens living abroad alone raised over 25 million dollars.

Although some mismanagement of funds has been reported via corruption and wasteful contracts to corrupt officials due to a lack of audit and public scrutiny, the project has been largely successful to date.

The plan of this trip was for Mr Solution to stay in Burao for 5 days, as agreed with the female travel companion, then return to Mogadishu, but this plan changed and his stay became 5 and a half years, due to events that happened.

Reaching Burao in the evening, they were greeted by family members in Mr Solution's family house. Tea and snacks were shared, then it was bedtime, although various people were coming over as they heard Mr Solution had finally arrived in Burao.

The following weeks were spent socialising with family members and opposition politicians of Mr Solution's political views, particularly the unity and reconciliation work done and still being worked on by Mr Solution and likeminded individuals.

One morning, Mr Solution got up early to see a private medical practice in Burao opened and run by a Somali internal medicine doctor who had worked in Germany for the past 30 years but returned to his country of birth. Upon his return to town, he met a fellow East African from Ethiopia who had been working as a medical technician at that practice in the laboratory department. After a brief introduction, contact numbers were exchanged, and a few days later, a meeting was arranged at his rented house near his work address. After lunch, some khat was ordered and a swift delivery was made to Debebe's house. Most of the day was spent listening to some Ethiopian and Somali music and chewing the khat, while discussing the situations in Ethiopia and Somalia.

After a while, Mr Solution came to understand this gentleman Debebe was more than a medical technician and defiantly worked for the Ethiopian government in some capacity. However, Mr Solution did not say this to him. Instead, Mr solution suggested how important it was for East African countries to turn the page on past history and hostilities and cooperate on economic and security issues holding East Africa back from fulfilling their potential so they can prosper together if the political climate is changed with new ideas and policies. Mr Solution said, "Don't you think it's time we bring Eritrea inside from the cold and end the long-standing war between your countries? This would greatly improve the lives of all citizens in both countries through trade, the mistrust would end, Eritreans fleeing and dying in the deadly migration to Europe would cease, and the destabilising rebels, given arms and bases by both sides, also affecting Somalia, would be repatriated to their respective countries without fear.

Djibouti and Eritrea would also benefit as you know they do not have normal diplomatic relations since they also had a war on their side of the border, where hostages captured are still held by both countries."

Debebe said, "Yes, I agree completely, but how do we do this?" Mr Solution said, "Well, the first part is done as we just discussed this and agreed it's the right thing to do. I will mention this to some people I know who could liaise with the decision-makers in these countries, including mine, and you should do the same however possible with your Ethiopian colleagues."

Mr Solution had a large social media following due to his political, reconciliation and peace-making activities online via Facebook and Twitter, which included an Eritrean who used to work in the same company as Mr Solution while in London. Also, a neighbour who was a strong follower of all matters concerning Eritrea, his birth country. Mr Solution purposely wrote on Twitter and Facebook about his idea of bringing Eritrea inside from the cold and ending the war with Ethiopia, knowing that this person would take note of the proposal and discuss it with his fellow Eritreans, particularly those he did military service with in his country., Then, since Eritrea is a closed country where the state has a tight grip on all matters, this type of idea would easily reach those in power quickly.

Mr Solution was convinced they would embrace this plan if presented, as it originated from a Somali man from Somalia and not from an Ethiopian, as the fear and mistrust held against one another were too great due to the 30-year war between them costing more than 100,000 lives.

Ethiopia had a new federal constitution based on ethnic regional states and there had been a major uprising and conflicts in the largest populated Oromo region, Amharic regions and the large Somali regions due to political grievances held against the long-ruling trigrey leadership. Political changes were needed urgently or the country was in danger of collapsing into anarchy and war which was a serious threat to Africa as a whole, particularly East Africa. Mr Solution and others were determined to steady the ship by all doing their bit. Some months later, a new prime minister named Abiy Ahmed was elected, via the ruling EPRDF party, who originated from the Oromo region, to stabilise the country, particularly the Oromo regions, as he was previously the region's president.

Straight away, the new prime minister presented plans to reform Ethiopian politics and adopt the plans made in Somalia by Mr Solution to make peace between Eritrea and Ethiopia.

Today, Prime Minister Abiy Ahmed is a Nobel peace prize winner for normalising diplomatic relations with Eritrea, bringing political dissidents such as armed rebels inside from Eritrea and elsewhere, freeing political prisoners in Ethiopia, and implementing political policies that previous leaders had failed to do for a long time.

It was now coming up to the end of 2013. Mr Solution was still in Northern Somalia because financial pressures, political pressures and social pressures were used against him so he did not return to Mogadishu to continue his work.

The passport of Mr Solution and a mobile SIM card used to receive funds via the mobile money operating in the country had been confiscated and hidden by family members in his own house, meaning his ability to exercise financial freedom to travel was hindered.

Mr Solution contacted some friends abroad to send him some funds via the Somali money transfer used over there and one said, "No problem; I will send you $5000 tomorrow, so go and collect it the day after."

Three days passed and no funds were received, which Mr Solution thought strange, so he contacted his friend who said the money transfer company owned by Somalis was being very difficult and refusing to accept the money and he didn't know why. "At what stage did this happen?" asked Mr Solution." "It happened when I gave them the receivers name, your name."

Mr Solution understood why they were doing this as the owners of the business and large numbers of his employees were from Hargeisa or Burao, northern Somalia, and had different political views to Mr Solution. In addition to them being very tribally aligned to the separatist's opinion of breaking away from Somalia due to business interests done with the Somaliland administration, their customer base was in northern Somalia mainly, and they had been using them exclusively for over 25 years since the country's banking system and national financial institutions ceased to function internationally, allowing money remittances to be an important player in connecting the country with funds outside it.

Mr Solution felt like he was in an open prison while time was passing by. One day, Mr Solution decided that if these dirty obstacles were put in front boxing him in, he should start to fight from inside to land the big shots that would bring the desired results for his political aspirations.

After a frantic search, 200 dollars hidden previously in a little compartment of his travel bag was found, enabling Mr Solution to travel to a province called Awdal, whose provincial capital is Borama. The plan was for Mr Solution to visit the local people there to gauge their views on the political direction or path they were being pushed along and to visit a university where students from various parts of Somalia studied.

Using two cars to get to Borama, Mr Solution arrived there around 9 pm after travelling for most of the day.

He checked into a hotel called Ontario after receiving the contact information to make the booking from two young students returning to university, who travelled all the way from a place called Gaalka'ayo, Mudug province.

Mr Solution wanted to see the local people and the sights, while also visiting a student whom Mr Solution assisted financially in going to university there.

It was well known that the people in this province did not share the view of becoming a separate country from the rest of Somalia but felt like they were being forced by political and military pressure to comply.

Mr Solution spent around 5 days in Borama, visiting the main attraction of the city, which is its decent university, where the students, from all parts of Somalia, were helping to support the local economy by renting property and shopping locally.

Most days, he ate out in restaurants, as the Ontario Hotel did not have a restaurant. One day, after lunch in the Awdal restaurant, Mr Solution was looking for a place to spend the rest of the day, so, he found a nice place behind the hotel buildings where local tribal chiefs and politically-minded men were sitting in large qaaci-style seating, chewing khat, and drinking sweet tea prepared by this colourful lady who invited Mr Solution to sit and enjoy a chewing session with the locals as she noticed he was from out of town. "Perfect, thanks. Exactly what I have been looking for."

Mr Solution introduced himself as a man from Burao visiting this lovely place, praising their pro-Somalia patriotism, peacefulness, and welcoming attitude towards students from all parts of the country while building integration and, above all, protecting the unity of Somalia while standing up to those who use bullying tactics to mute their voices.

Mr Solution returned to Burao after 5 days away, not stopping in Hargeisa overnight but passing through. Not long after this trip, there were disputes with the local administration in Borama from local citizens angered by two young boys who had been shot dead inside a football stadium by the Somaliland police unjustly. Apparently, their crime was that the boys played the national anthem of Somalia on speakers causing the whole stadium to stand up and sing along.

Following this terrible incident, deadly demonstrations followed with the burning of a police station and the governor's house. Several police officers were killed and the governor and his son narrowly escaped and fled the city. An armed rebel group headed by a chief named Suldan Wabbar was announced some weeks later.

One particular morning, Mr Solution was having his usual espresso in a coffee shop on the west side of Burao, when a lively discussion started between the customers regarding events that happened in Borama. One customer, who Mr Solution called 'the hater who does not know why he hates' shouted loudly, "I think it was you behind all this, as you just returned from Borama not long ago on a mysterious visit," pointing at Mr Solution.

Sitting next to him were police officers, one in uniform with three stars on either side of his shoulder, who must be plainclothes officers observing.

Mr Solution laughed and said, "Can you prove it, Mr Hater who does not know why he hates? Mr Solution is a people's man who goes wherever the good people are." A loud burst of laughter erupted from people in the cafeteria. An old man named Jirde, who was a geography teacher previously but had to take reluctant retirement due to severe back problems, said, "Mr Solution has a point; any response?"

Mr Hater looked angry and defeated so swiftly got up and said, "See you around".

This coffee shop was popular with Mr Solution and many visitors to Burao from other parts of Somalia. It is located near the provincial authority's compound where work activities were busy from 7 am until 12:30 pm, then all workers disappeared for the rest of the day.

Because of the nature of Mr Solution's work putting the jumbled jigsaw pieces of a nation together, no political offices were opened for the political party he created. It was all done in informal settings such as restaurants, hotels, cafés and other social meeting places or via the internet using emails or social media. The reason why Mr Solution adopted this strategy was because it would not attract attention, causing serious political or security issues, while giving him the space to connect the dots of this construction.

Mr Solution was seen as a people's person by the public as he mingled with all regardless of background or status. He shared jokes, ideas and resources and was not afraid to get his hands dirty to help out when needed.

This evening, around 9 pm, walking home from the other side of town after spending the day chewing khat with a friend in a big two-storey compound owned by a lady who lives abroad. The main house was empty, but the watchman, who also did the gardening, lived in the guest house.

Passing the old cemetery near an area called Taweli, Mr Solution noticed a man squatting, defecating on a gravesite. He stopped and said, "Hey, do you know that is a grave below you?" He replied, "Carry on walking, man, I am busy." Something snapped in Mr Solution, who quickly walked up to the man who was still squatting and slapping him in the face twice. "Do you know you are dumping human shit on a dead person's grave?"

Mr Solution dragged the person along the road for a while until he escaped the grip of Mr Solution's hand and ran into the dark night.

That night, Mr Solution found it hard to sleep while thinking about the fight he had with the disrespectful man, and what to do about those cemeteries, which did not have gates to protect them or any cleaning maintenance done. So, early in the morning, after the fajr morning prayer in a mosque, Mr Solution started with the imam of the main old 150-year-old mosque, called the jaama masjid, informing the imam of the conditions of these cemeteries, and how people urinate and poo on them, all because they do not have gates around them to protect them..

Mr Solution said, "Imam, if we do not fix this now, tomorrow they will defecate on your grave too. Talk about it in your sermons and let's start raising resources to construct fences around all the cemeteries around the city." The imam said, "Do you know you are the first person to raise this concern?" Next, Mr Solution travelled to the largest money transfer offices in the city and, after a brief chat with some of the employees, requested an account to be opened to collect money which would be used to construct gates around the neglected cemeteries in Burao. He said, "Here is my first contribution of 10 dollars to the account." He then left immediately.

Next day, a meeting with the management of the largest mobile network operator was planned. Mr Solution went to his office to request a mobile money account opened in the name of Burao Cemetery, also advising this company not to just be profit-seekers collecting money from the people but also to be a responsible conscientious company, willing to give back to the community by giving funds to build institutions, community projects, such as this one, and educational projects, as that would provide them with fantastic positive marketing campaigns.

The local authority felt threatened when they heard about this project, independently put together by Mr Solution. They were puzzled by him as he had come from London, via Mogadishu, and was involved in national politics and nation-building and whose opinions they did not share. This plan was being completely funded by the citizens, with businesses contributing however much they could donate, so immediately, the local authority announced that they would be building walls around the old cemeteries and future ones to protect them against land been stolen and the dumping of waste and all funds raised currently would be managed by the local authority who would use it for the project.

Burao had struggled with religiously motivated groups in the past who wanted to control and govern, but the truth is their motivation was nothing to do with religion. It was a facade to cover up the gathering of financial assets. They loved the money and wished to capture all resources to dominate the people while keeping them poor and in need of their assistance.

Still, these groups were very active and had large businesses. Some of these individuals had left for southern Somalia to join and become top leaders in the terrorist group Al-Shabaab, but the majority of their families, including wives, still lived in the city, meaning they could come and go as they pleased without any checks by the authorities. For a long time, they had infiltrated the authorities in all sectors, even creating a religious police force under the banner of "stopping the bad and delivering the good".

A minibus with large speakers went all around the city with posters attached to its roof and side doors displaying a message which said they were raising funds to build a cemetery wall. Those in the bus were collecting cash donations and mobile wallet payments but nobody was sure who they worked for or was bothering to investigate.

Large donations from the Diaspora, some as much as 10,000 dollars, were received towards the building of the wall. Six months later, a wall stretching around 7 kilometres for the old large cemetery was finished, as announced by the big bearded mayor of the province, claiming all the credit, although it was clearly known whose idea and plan it was from the beginning.

Mr Solution knew that more than 250,000 dollars had been raised since the project started but only around 50% had been spent on the project, with the rest stolen via corrupt channels, but he was happy something had been achieved while teaching the people how they could collectively build things of national interest with unity and participation and not waiting for handouts from NGOs and governments.

Chapter 5.
Empowering Discriminated Tribes Politically, Economically and Socially

While in northern Somalia, Mr Solution was spending a lot of time with unjustly marginalised or discriminated groups or tribes. He ate with them when some members of the Somali tribes thought it was forbidden or uncustomary to do so. He also attended and enjoyed their wedding parties to show those racist people, borne out of ignorance and fake folklore stories, that they are not different from them and that these wrong beliefs spread about them are fake and the time to correct these errors is now.

These tribe's professions were barbershop owners, hair salon owners, shoemakers or repairers, metal workers such as knife, pots and pan-makers or welders, and tailors. Basically, they were the important, yet undervalued, skilled or technical workers of the community.

Mr Solution planned to empower them politically, economically and socially by getting involved with them and giving them ideas and plans to overcome this. Mr Solution was regarded as a people's man who was able to interact with them on all levels as he did not care what some members of other communities thought.

Mr Solution had become good friends with his barber and told him how all the barbers should open a cooperative account and put some money each month into it to enable them to buy business equipment in bulk abroad, making it cheaper for them and also making them the main suppliers of their businesses.

This plan worked successfully. Then, he moved to political empowerment ideas by showing how, in Mogadishu, women were given a 30% parliamentary quota and their fellow tribesmen in southern Somalia were given full ministerial positions, and since elections were scheduled in the Somaliland region where three political parties were to contest the elections, it was only right their field candidates became active on T.V stations and radio, especially with the nationalist opposition party.

A strong campaign was launched after this by their tribal chiefs and kings, highlighting the injustices of the past which needed to be corrected.

One day, Mr Solution was having lunch with a man in a restaurant. He said, "Hey, man, you have a nice fine shirt, jacket and trousers on, but a very old, tired-looking pair of shoes; why?" Mr Solution said, "These shoes are special to me. They have been loyal to me for six years, taking me to ten provinces of Somalia, and keeping my unjustly discriminated skilled shoe repairer going so he can provide for his family. These shoes have a history which should be told, or maybe someday they should be put in a museum."

There was conflict between two communities who lived in the same district, about 140 kilometres away from the district capital of Togdheer. The conflict had its original routes in a difference of political opinion; one community had no aspirations to be part of the local Somaliland government as it supported the central federal government of Somalia, and the other was pro-Somaliland administration. So, because of these two opposing views, the situation was exploited by politicians who wished to control this district by causing tribal fighting, then they used its military forces to back one side to capture the district.

So, these local nomadic men were given funds by individuals from North West province to dig boreholes in the opposing community's villages.

This triggered a war between the clans which lasted more than two years, with lots of casualties on both sides.

One day, while in the middle of town on his way to the usual coffee shop for his morning macchiato,

Mr Solution received news from a very angry man saying there had been six killings and many injured by an attack in the conflict zone of his clansmen and he would be gathering truckloads of armed men from the city to go there and avenge their deaths. He said, "You and your tribe, who are known for fighting, should join us if you are leaders of this clan".

This man was erratic and angry, with an AK47 in his hand, waving it around in the direction of Mr Solution who reacted by grabbing the gun off the man as it could have easily fired and hit him. "Listen here, you silly fool, there is a saying - your neighbour is closer than your clan – so, I will try and bring a ceasefire, peace and reconciliation between you brotherly communities and end this senseless war created by the men you are supporting who truly don't care about you but are using you for their own political ventures. I should keep this gun as it's the law here that since I took it off you by force as you were pointing It at me in a threatening manner, I should take it. However, I don't want it, so take it back and goodbye."

As this was in the middle of town, people stopped to look and gathered around the heated argument. Mr Solution walked away, saying, "Nothing to see here, folks, just two friends having a family chat, so go about your business".

Mr Solution finally arrived at the coffee shop and called the waiter over and said, "Give me a double today. Bring some snacks too." It was a very hot day, the dry humid time when the tropical rainy season was approaching. Mr Solution was sweating as the clouds were hovering above, looking like the Heavens were about to open.

Mr Solution called a friend in Mogadishu to ask for the number for an elder, who was also a tribal leader, who they met there while electing the new Somali parliament representatives, to discuss coming over to northern Somalia so that finally, this conflict could be sorted and squashed. Mr Solution then made a second call to family members and tribe members who lived in the neighbouring district of the conflict area, ordering them not to take sides and get involved in the conflict between the clans next door, but to play a peacekeeping role by relocating, with their livestock, to land and villages between the two warring tribes, keeping them apart until a reconciliation meeting could be arranged. They agreed to relocate, using their camels as transport and, by the grace of God, the tropical rainy season started first in the new location they were settling in. For a period of three weeks, there was peace without any incidents.

Sitting at the table next to Mr Solution was a man with a small Hitler-style moustache who had been listening to all the calls Mr Solution made. He was an old Soviet-trained spy who worked for the government in the region. However, Mr Solution knew this and deliberately spoke in a loud tone so he would hear all that was said and could report it to his superiors. They would then scramble all the elders of the region and resources to arrange a quick meeting of the warring sides, fearing how this independent Mr Solution had taken the initiative which would give him the support of the ordinary population, allowing him to promote his own political views and policies. The local administration was afraid of this, as their strategy had been to silence, discredit and isolate Mr Solution, personally and politically.

The wife of one of the elders informed Mr Solution they had left Mogadishu and arrived in Hargeisa to travel to their home town as the peace and reconciliation meeting was being held in the coming weeks. It just so happened to be being held in the little village of Mr Solution's grandfather.

The meeting was arranged quickly, as expected by the regional administrator, and they reached a peaceful resolution, which still holds today in 2020, after these events 6 years ago.

The local authority's employees, such as minsters, civil servants and even the regional president, were known to Mr Solution as some were individuals from the Diaspora who used to reside in the same city abroad. Some were distant relatives who worked there in some capacity, while others were jealous rivals spooked by the influcnce Mr Solution had built up while having a relaxed, calm, independent hand and unknown different approaches to their usual tactics.

Due to their paranoia, some said that Mr Solution was a British operative, as the status quo was changing rapidly for the benefit of the population. One day, while having a chewing session in a tribal elders meeting, a rude old man said, "I think we have been unknowingly dancing to your songs lately but we are going to shut you down soon, young man; soon."

Mr Solution replied, "It is democratic times we are living in, so good luck. A healthy opposition is good, but remember, don't play dirty, old man, as I seem to be catching the mud and rocks you have kept throwing at me lately and throwing them back at your faces and, at this rate, you will have no faces to face me."

Mr Solution was not an orthodox religious man, but he had faith and participated in the main obligatory Islamic activities, such as daily prayer, fasting in the month of Ramadan, doing good deeds and giving to charity and had performed his hajj pilgrimage in the past so had a decent knowledge of the faith.

So, a plan against Mr Solution was created, using some of his family members who worked for the Somaliland authorities, to grab him and take him to a religious nuthouse. This was a place where people who need genuine medical assistance, whether it's physical or mental, but cannot afford it, or innocent ignorant people who think Islam has all the answers to everything, are kept for months if not years all paid in US dollars by their manipulated relatives.

In broad daylight in the middle of town, a car carrying 6 men approached Mr Solution and the men get out and physically grabbed him.

Mr Solution was a little shocked but was expecting them to do something dirty like this when he refused to work for the Somaliland authorities as had been suggested by some family and tribe members.

There were loud arguments and tussles and Mr Solution head-butted one of the attackers causing a bloody nose. Then, all of a sudden, Mr Solution became extremely calm as he realised this was exactly what they wanted, for him to became upset and fight them in the middle of town and them saying he was mad and they had to do this for his own good, so he said, "I will go with you to see the religious cleric at his centre. He can read the Quran on me to prove I am not possessed by evil and no evil eye has been done to me as you wrongly say. However, I want the cleric to read the Quran on all of you as well; do we have a deal?"

They agreed and arrived at the centre. There was a queue of fully veiled women with appointment cards in their hands, waiting for the cleric just like a medical practice, but this wasn't one. Some of the resident patients were outside in the courtyard, including two men originally from the UK. Mr Solution recognised one. He was a tall, skinny, frail-looking man who came over and shook hands, saying, "How are you? And what are you doing here?" "It's a long story, friend. You look different but I still remember you." "Yes, twelve years of being here with these people does that to you. Listen, keep your head down, stay calm and you should leave in 30 minutes. I am here because I have been fighting them from the beginning, as they robbed me of all the assets I inherited from my father, such as houses, land and businesses, and they ganged up on me driving me insane in and out of this nuthouse."

"Ok, thanks for the heads up, man. When I return, I will inform the British government your passport has expired and you have been kept in Burao for over 10 years against your will."

He entered the cleric's office and explained there was nothing wrong with me but that it was a deliberate forced act by these fellows who had been paid by opposing individuals of mine to do this trick for political reasons. He asked the cleric to please read the beautiful holy Quran on him, but also on these guys as their behaviour had been very abnormal.

The cleric smiled, sprayed some water on Mr Solution's face, read the Quran loudly in his ear and said, "It's all finished. This man is fine but I recommend you buy these herbs for 10 dollars." "No thanks, sheik. Can you also read the Quran on these gentlemen and I will pay their fees?" All of a sudden, they ran off in a hurry saying, "We are done, goodbye."

Mr Solution left the place about 20 minutes later, much to the disappointment of those who had planned this terrible experience who were watching outside.

Not happy with this dirty low thing experienced by Mr Solution and the abuse of people in these religious nuthouses by unregulated money-motivated individuals exploiting the people, Mr Solution decided these bad practices must be highlighted. Firstly, a religious cleric was arrested and sent to prison, and his place in Burao was closed down when a mentally sick woman who sought help was found to be pregnant by the cleric who took advantage of the sick women.

A religious school in Hargeisa city designed for Somali girls born in the EU, Canada, and the USA, who had been returned to the country for what's known as cultural repatriation by their parents, had been in the news headlines. Usually, their mothers paid to leave them there for Islamic teachings in the hope that it would improve their behaviour. The authorities in the girls' country of birth became aware after one young girl detained there stole a phone and contacted the embassy of her country. So, a planeload of officials arrived to take the girls back and close the school down. These places had been created specifically for young Somalis born abroad, as their parents had hard currency to pay with and they had been contacted by the owners of these centres advising that they could turn their children into reformed, well-behaved, Islamic-educated children.

Some of Mr Solution's like-minded friends, who became aware of this incident in Burao, sent over a religious cleric named the Sprayer, from a coastal city called Bosaso. He arranged large gatherings of people in football stadiums and outside spaces, spraying them with large hosepipes from water trucks to cleanse their demons using holy water.

So, one day, while back in the tribal elders' meeting and socialising house, Mr Solution said to the old man who was previously threatening him, "It appears the Somaliland political ideology and supporters are possessed by the devil or voodoo, as you can see on the TV channels that people are in hysterics, falling to the floor when Sheik the Sprayer is treating them. Look at the TV, Mister!"

He kept silent as he knew his dirty tricks had come back to him and his community, just like Mr Solution warned him before.

Some months later, Mr Solution had encountered some family members doing things they should not be doing in his family house and had become very upset by it, causing loud arguments and waking the neighbours. Threats were made to Mr Solution that the corrupt police would be paid to arrest him, although it was his house and the troublemakers were family members who lived there free of charge.

Mr Solution decides to leave as the situation could get out of control as one of the family members had a large knife and was waving it around in a threatening manner. Walking down the road, a young guy who was also a relative ran after Mr Solution and said, "Your cousin's house in the next street is empty as the family moved out temporarily, so, let's get you the keys to stay there tonight." The keys were fetched and Mr Solution spent the night in this empty house but returned to his own home the following day. However, he kept the keys for some months, sometimes staying there to look after the home until its owners returned.

One night, after a late night out, Mr Solution decided to stay at the empty house. Waking up in the morning, he saw the ashes of a fire on the front door and wall. The fire had been started deliberately by somebody while Mr Solution was sleeping, with the intention of burning the house down with him inside.

'This was an arson attack,' thought Mr Solution. 'Thank God it failed and I am alive.' He summoned the man whose family lived there to witness it and make a police report; however, he became silent and refused to report it to the police.

The following day, Mr Solution informed a police officer at the station of the incident. He said, This sounds like an attempted terrorist attack but we cannot do anything if the house owner does not wish to report it.

Mr Solution returned that evening to the same house, knocking on the door of the neighbour on the right, who had many kids, to ask if he knew anything about the fire being started under the front door of the house. He said he had not seen anything. Then, the neighbour directly opposite was approached. "Did you see anyone last night on our street?" The lady said, "No".

The owner of the house arrived, so Mr Solution decided to go to the house that night to collect some of his belongings. On entering, he heard a noise at the back of the house near the kitchen. When he investigated further, Mr Solution found a goat locked in the toilet. He called the house owner who was sitting outside the door, "Come here! You won't believe what I just found locked in the toilet; look!" Sweating and puffing heavily on a cigarette, he appeared confused, but Mr Solution thought he knew something about this and said, "Look, I am gone. Here are the keys to your weird house. Maybe we should call the Sprayer to the house as there are strange activities here".

Some days later, Mr Solution, while buying milk from the local shop, was making jokes about a goat that had wings who somehow found itself locked in a toilet of a 5-bedroom bungalow then a teenage kid, whose family recently moved to the same street said, "That goat you're talking about was our goat and we don't know how it got into that house either as it was locked from the outside with a padlock."

Mr Solution said to the shopkeeper, "Hey, make sure my milk is not goat. I don't want to grow wings and end up in strange places this evening. Remember, I ordered fresh camel milk".

The kid said, "In case you did not know, the house has a separate garage door with a single room rented by a fat short woman with two kids. Her husband is a soldier; I have seen them all." On hearing this information, Mr Solution discovers this was true, meaning these people who rented the garage with a room were involved in this along with some relatives who had knowledge of this plot but kept quiet. The next day, Mr Solution passed the house and knocked on the garage door. There was no answer; the neighbour opposite said, "They moved out yesterday in a hurry".

It was quite clear to Mr Solution that the poor woman with the two little girls and some extended relatives were made to do this by others who paid or manipulated them, as Mr Solution did not play the tribal card like them or share their racist views.

Since this incident and some terrible little mind games being played by the local politicians and very inward primitive tribal or religiously motivated people, he decided to focus more, and be alert to his environment for safety reasons.

It was midday in February 2018. Mr Solution was in the middle of the city returning from a meeting with his friend the retired geography teacher and elders, discussing the results of the regional presidential elections of Somaliland, where large numbers of the population who voted were complaining, saying it was a blatant theft by the incoming president with help from a company belonging to the UAE who had been given the contract to count the votes with their equipment. After hours discussing this along with other matters, Mr Solution left for midday prayer and lunch.

Occasionally, Mr Solution, without prior planning, went into various restaurants apart from his regular coffee joint to eat and drink, checking out the quality. He usually ordered a bowl of soup, then a plate of rice with meat with a few roasted vegetables or a little salad on it. This was unusual, as most people in the city don't eat salads or vegetables. He got up to wash his hands as he would be eating with his hands like the locals. Upon returning to the table, he saw a man sitting at the opposite side of the table with a fake smile. The food had already arrived and the man opposite had ordered the same food as Mr Solution but without the salad or vegetables on it. Mr Solution noticed some white-looking capsules of powder on the salad and the man opposite was acting strangely, smiling at Mr Solution.

Mr Solution was concerned by what he had seen on his plate but kept calm and did not eat it. There was a noisy argument outside the restaurant. Mr Solution said loudly, "Gosh, what is that? "then calmly switched the plates of food while the man was looking away, giving him his own medicine. Mr Solution ate quickly with his hands, enjoying the food, and said, "The cook has prepared tasty food today, do you not think?" The man opposite smiled and said, "Yes, delicious. Don't leave any on the plate." Mr Solution gobbled down the food, licking his fingers clean of the sauce.

When it was time to pay, Mr Solution paid in the local currency and picked up a toothpick, observing the man opposite as he was struggling to pay using his mobile wallet account and was sweating, appearing in distress. Mr Solution went outside to light a cigarette. With his two-dollar Ray-Ban sunglasses on, the dodgy-looking man exited, looking at Mr Solution in amazement, and tried to walk away, but he kept falling down as if he had tripped over something. Mr Solution went over to help him up and said, "Are you ok? What's wrong? I hope you have not been drinking alcohol in this heat; its potency will hit you, man".

The man looks distressed but said nothing as he looked away and continued to walk, falling and stumbling often. Mr Solution was convinced the man was trying to poison or drug him but karma got him and gave him his own medicine. That was the last time Mr Solution saw this man.

Many of the local council officials and policemen in the provincial capital were known to Mr Solution. Some months after the last incident, while he was walking home for lunch, there was a protest and rocks were being thrown at the main offices of the city's disliked electricity company which had a monopoly on the supply of electricity for the whole province. He stopped and asked a bystander what was happening. He told him that these women and men were protesting as several people had been killed last night by these dangerous wires hanging everywhere.

Mr Solution shouted, "Bloodsuckers!" then was about to walk away when a police officer, who worked as a security guard for the electricity company's offices, along with two others, approached Mr Solution and grabbed him, saying "You, get in this car".

Mr Solution was driven in a police car by the hated and corrupt police commander of the station, who had been involved in many killings of people inside the police station, including a registered disabled British man who was also a citizen on holiday. When he knowingly allowed four men to enter the police cell, he was being kept in for an incident some days earlier, these men tortured him to death then the police covered it up.

This corrupt police commander was also on the payroll of several big companies in the city who paid him monthly salaries to do their dirty work and supply police officers as security guards.

On arrival, Mr Solution was registered, his mobile, cash, belt, shoelaces and pen were removed and he was given the number 1420 written on his belongings.

Mr Solution asked, "Why have I been arrested?" The young officer at the counter said, "Take him to cell 1." Mr Solution was taken to a cell with seven other people, including four young boys who were between 12 and 14 years old and two middle-aged men. There were no toilets, and the prisoners told him they used the water bottles to urinate in when needed and had to beg the police officers to use the only usable hole when desperate to relieve themselves.

There were no beds, only plastic strew like worn-out mats on the concrete floor for the prisoners to sit or sleep on. Mr Solution briefly chatted to fellow prisoners in the cell to find out why they were there and got various different answers, most saying they were innocent of wrongdoing. One asked "Why are you here? What have you done?" Mr Solution replied "I don't know and have done nothing. Hopefully, these idiots will tell me".

It was now late in the evening when all the prisoners were removed from their cells and taken into the lobby for the handover of the night shift workers at the station. As the prisoners were being called by their names, the corrupt police commander started attacking a young prisoner coming out of his cell late by hitting him with the back of his AK47, while another officer joined in with a traditional stick called a budh, which looked like a baseball bat, injuring the detainee severely. Mr Solution looked around to see if anybody would stop the assault or say something, but it was all silent as if this was a regular thing, so Mr Solution said, "Stop! That is very wrong!" The attack on the prisoner suddenly stopped and the attackers came past Mr Solution on the way to the front bench. One of the policemen asked, "Who said that"? A prisoner replied, "Said what?" And they carried on calling the names of the prisoners and why they had been arrested. Then came the turn of Mr Solution. "Your name and why you're here?" Mr Solution replied "I've done nothing wrong and don't know why I have been wrongfully arrested. I was hoping you could tell me since it was your colleagues who arrested me."

Shortly afterwards, the prisoners returned to their cells. One officer approached Mr Solution and asked, "Do you want to call your family to let them know you are here, or your tribal chief to get you out?" He was doing this purposely to see if Mr Solution would get upset and emotional, resorting to using tribal dynamics to free him, but Mr Solution replied, "No thanks. I am sure you will do the right thing by letting me out ASAP." He was returned to the holding cell.

Mr Solution spent a very uncomfortable night in the shared cell. Next morning breakfast was brought in by family members of the prisoners. It was shared by all the cellmates. Mr Solution reluctantly had a little taste with a hot cup of tea from a flask. At midday, Mr Solution noticed these actors, who had familiar faces, sitting and smoking outside in the courtyard, looking very suspicious. A second night was spent in the cell. Some of the detainees had been released as some had only been sent there by foes to get information on Mr Solution's behaviour during this time in prison.

On the second day, Mr Solution needed the toilet, so he banged the cell door loudly to get the attention of one of the police officers to let him out. When the officer arrived, Mr Solution recognised him from a district outside of the province. The one usable toilet was not fit for purpose and he asked him, "Is there another toilet?" He said, "Come, there is one outside within the compound used by the police and women prisoners." On the way to the outside toilet, there were women sitting under a tree and a police officer fighting with a prisoner who was chained at the legs and arms while some other officers were sitting watching, chewing the drug called khat. Mr Solution broke up the fight, separating them, then got a bucket of water with a plastic bottle to clean himself in the toilet as there was no toilet paper. The toilet is what's known as a 'toad in the hole', where one must remove clothes then squat to use it.

Walking back through the courtyard to the cell, a tall slim woman shouted the name of Mr Solution. Mr Solution looked over. "Yes, hello and you are?" She introduced herself as an extended relative. "What are you doing here? This is no place for a lady." "I have been arrested for fighting these ladies in the market," she said. "Don't you remember my auntie from Hargeisa who was phoning you when you were in Mogadishu to leave and come here?" "Yes, I recall now. So, your auntie was calling me here to be jailed for no reason?" She smiled and with a look of embarrassment, said, "No, this is where your people are." "If that is the case, where are they? I have been locked up in this place for two days now without any visits and I don't see the city burning in anger about this wrongful arrest. What happened to the saying, 'if relatives help each other, what evil can hurt them'?

"I think my people are in Mogadishu. The ones who wrongly put me here are political enemies using my so-called families, not the family and communities I have been supporting and teaching for over 20 years." He then left to return to the cell with the police officer.

On the third day, Mr Solution was released without any charges or explanation as to why he had been imprisoned for 3 days and nights. His personal belongings were collected. Then he took a trip to the shop to purchase packets of cigarettes, drinks, and food for the remaining prisoners he shared the cell with for three days. The delivery was made to them with a message to one of the officers to look at the case of one prisoner who had special needs, then he headed home to shower and eat the takeaway food purchased along the way and to try and get information about who was behind this wrongful arrest.

Mr Solution remembered that, on the day of his arrest, an old police officer, who was first cousin to the president of the separatist regime, was coming out of the offices of the electricity company while the demonstrations were in progress and a council member, nicknamed 'the son of the barefoot man', formally resident in the EU, who knew of Mr Solution's political activities and views but was strongly against them, was standing almost next to Mr Solution with his son when the police officers appeared unexpectedly and arrested him after he shouted "BLOODSUCKERS" to the electricity company and the crying women repeated it in the demonstrations. This was what had triggered his arrest.

Mr Solution had looked back as he was getting into the car. The local councillor had a smirking grin on his face towards Mr Solution, so it eventually became clear that he and the administration he worked for were behind this wrongful arrest, due to unfounded fear surrounding Mr Solution's work.

The electricity company had been reported on the Somali T.V stations as being unsafe, with dangerous live wires dangling everywhere, causing many houses and businesses to burn. The company was unregulated by the authorities as corrupt deals to secure a monopoly as the only energy provider had been done with them. This included winning, unchallenged, large amounts of solar energy farm equipment funded by the EU for rural towns, schools, villages, and hospitals, but diverted to them by the authorities when company officials paid large bribes to government officials.

Fighting corruption was of paramount importance to Mr Solution, as it was a major problem in the country, keeping the citizens poor and denying them the opportunities to prosper, so the above incident had become headline news. The headlines also covered the alleged investment in the ports of Berbera and Bosaso by a company owned by a middle-eastern government, without the knowledge of the sovereign federal government of Somalia or any due process, but arranged via corrupt channels such as paying large bribes to businessmen and local regional administrators. At the time, there were demonstrations by the public against this and it was globally reported as a completely corrupt arrangement, dangerous to the security and stability of a fragile country which was making a decent recovery.

Mr Solution was also publicly against this so-called investment, but in reality, it was a rip-off of a deal, considered null and void legally, causing public outrage. A year later, outside his office, the port manager, appointed by a foreign government, was killed in the port city of Bosaso.

Via his political party website and social media web pages with a variety of large influential followers, including human rights groups, international governments, government officials of the federal government of Somalia who previously helped this separatist regime obtain certain funds for development and humanitarian purposes, Mr Solution displayed information, shared pictures and wrote about the terrible corruption, pictures of children behind bars taken when he himself was in prison as he was leaving the police station, the arrest of political party members, hundreds of journalist's and activists, the support for terrorist groups by individuals and human rights abuses of children and women in jails by this separatist regime in northern Somalia. Knowledge of these flagrant violations resulted in the immediate cessation of funding.

Mr Solution believed the terrible wrong-doings such as arrests of journalists, opposition political party members, abuse of citizens by this rough regime on him and hundreds of others, would now decrease as they would take notice by stopping this. at least for a short period of time and little changes of attitude appeared with the release of arrested individuals, including children.

Mr Solution met a friend who had recently arrived in the country from abroad. He wanted to have a drive to a province contested by two rival administrations of the federal government 230 kilometres away from Togdheer. He was going for the day and needed company there and back. Mr Solution needed a change of scenery and gladly accepted.

A ten in the morning, the car set off on the long road which ran from the north to the south of the country, which passes through most provinces built by the overthrown socialist military regime in the late 1970s. The road was still in very good condition.

The friend was not a very good driver; a little amateurish, to be honest. Mr Solution had taught him how to drive abroad, using his own car, 10 years earlier, so was concerned. "Do you want me to drive?" asked Mr Solution. "No, I am fine, just be a good navigator for me." "Sure, just keep your eyes on the road. If a goat or wild animal steps on the road, don't swerve, just hit it head-on, if you can't stop."

They stopped at a little village along the way to purchase some khat, as it made the journey feel better and increased the driver's alertness. They arrived around 2 pm in Las Anod, or LA for short, which is the capital of the Sool province. They stopped at a food and drinks shop in the middle of town. As Mr Solution was purchasing a lahooh wrap, a young man approached and said, "I know you". Mr Solution turned around and he said, "I am your friend on Facebook and I heard your talk on the VOA Somali service with Zeynab about the politics of Somalia." Mr Solution was a little surprised as this person was a school kid, maybe 15 years old. "Yes, that was me, but how old are you? You have your school uniform on, so why were you listening to this boring stuff?" He said, "Yes, I am a school kid, but I know what's happening in the country. You are younger than all these old politicians who never retire, causing wars, always saying the same things but never doing anything for us young people and stealing our futures".

Mr Solution was impressed with the bravery and honesty of the kid, so he shook his hand and said, "Things are changing or have already changed as the young people like you have woken up and are demanding a new beginning. Well done; you are a clear example".

The driver was a big supporter of the separatist Somaliland administration who, by force, controlled this town and the majority of the province. He said, "Let's go, man." They had a quick drive around the town, then to a petrol station to obtain some fuel for the return trip. The driver was eager to leave the town as he appeared to dislike the attention Mr Solution was getting because of his friendly chats with the locals who liked his pragmatic views and philosophy of unity on things.

They started driving back to Burao when, 5 kilometres out, there was a checkpoint, with several police officers and a few locals under a little hut, checking all the vehicles coming in and going out. As they approached the metal bar, car and driver details were taken then the officer said, "Your road tax expired last month and we have fresh ones here so you have to purchase one if you want to carry on with your journey."

The driver was being very cocky and said, "It's only 2 days into the new month. I tried buying one in my home city but none were available and I don't have 60 dollars with me." The police officer would have let him drive off as he had been allowing many other cars through, but due to the driver's cocky, abusive manner, he said, "No, you will buy a new one if you want to go home tonight." Standing outside the car smoking a cigarette, Mr Solution said to the driver, "Since you are always banging on about this separatist regime, it's only fair you purchase a road tax and be a patriotic law-abiding citizen." The policeman agreed and laughed, saying, "You should listen to your diplomatic chief." Eventually, he phoned his businessman father to send him the money via his mobile wallet, then he paid for the road tax. The police officers, who were getting very upset with his attitude, said, "You're lucky I have not arrested you or pointed my AK at you."

They left the checkpoint after almost two hours. It was late in the evening and very dark as there was no street lighting. The driver insisted on driving, so Mr Solution was doing his best to make sure he did not make a silly mistake and crash. Then suddenly, he swerves the car, trying to avoid a pothole, almost tipping the car on its side as he lost control. Fortunately, they survived that, but a loud argument erupted between the driver and Mr Solution, who dragged the driver out of the car and drove the rest of the journey back, arrived home at around 11:45 pm.

Dal Barwaaqo & Dad Ka Baahan !

Dal walba, dadkiisaa dhisa !
SOMALIA

PRODUCE OF SOMALIA

XSS
Xisbiga Shacabka Somalia

MUQDISHO

MANDELA WAY SE1

Chapter 6.
Peace-keeping Tukaraq, Then Exiting.

A Somali proverb says, "It's not the man's age but his understanding." There is also another African proverb which says, "Where you will sit when you are old shows where you stood in youth," although the country of origin of this is unclear.

It was the beginning of 2019 and, for over 3 months, there had been a war raging in a little village on the main road towards Mogadishu via Garowe called Tukaraq. The province is Sool, and its provincial capital is Las Anod. It is a region contested for control by tribally aligned Somaliland administration and Puntland administration. Deadly tribal conflicts were frequent due to political support for the rival administrations starting the fire, the last one causing more than 170 deaths between two clans of the same tribe.

Mr Solution got a call, which this often happened when conflicts or serious political matters arose, from a reporter named Abdi Waahid, Dalsan radio station, based in Mogadishu, to discuss the escalating conflict. As Mr Solution's location was nearer, he asked him how the situation was and what should be done about it.

Mr Solution explained that the situation was very volatile, with daily clashes from the heavily armed military of both sides, and many casualties. An immediate ceasefire was needed firstly, then an intervention by the federal government of Somalia to bring the national army and federal police to maintain the peace by building a buffer zone. Unfortunately, the central federal government did not seize the opportunity due to weakness of leadership and lack of political will required.

The conflict was still raging and, if it was not stopped, could bring all-out war to northern Somalia, causing huge instability not seen in the last two decades in the region. Mr Solution was very concerned and decided to visit the region on a casual peace-making mission and sightseeing visit, as it had worked well in previous situations. He also submitted a Somali passport application to the immigration department located in Garowe, Nugaal province as it was the nearest one in northern Somalia due to the unreasonable policies of the Somaliland administration not to allow an office to be opened there.

Firstly, he took a 3-day trip to Hargeisa to purchase a plane ticket to London in the next months, while misdirecting some unwanted attention by people who had been following Mr Solution. He arrived in Hargeisa city and booked into a hotel on the west side of the city where the hotel owners and many usual guests were from the Sool province where this conflict was, to get further information of the situation and issues.

There was a travel agent and Bus Company office in the hotel, so Mr Solution enquired about the availability of plane tickets and found out the travel schedule for buses to Garowe via Tukaraq.

Sitting outside with a bus driver in front the hotel to cool down after returning to the hotel after a day of some shopping and chewing khat, a man with a large belly, appearing to look like a drunk man, came over asking peculiar questions to the bus driver. Mr Solution thought nothing of it but one of the other drivers said, "He is a spy working for the administration. Be careful with him. He tried to frame my friend for bringing alcohol to the city on his bus, when it was him who often brought it, through his connections from Ethiopia, by bribing the border police".

Mr Solution phoned a guy in Mogadishu to get a ticket for him to London on Turkish airlines from Mogadishu via Istanbul, but the following day, deliberately purchased another ticket, from an independent travel agent in the city centre, with Ethiopian Airlines, travelling from the Somali region of Ethiopia, Jigjiga city, via Bole Addis Ababa to London Heathrow scheduled for 3 months' time.

Mr Solution checked out of the hotel after 3 days and caught the bus back to Togdheer, Burao, with a planned trip to Garowe arranged with the bus driver from the hotel in Hargeisa.

He boarded the bus to Burao. It had a T.V screen showing local comedy actors from Burao. Mr Solution sat at the back of the half-full 50-seater bus. There was a young slim man who had a face familiar to Mr Solution but he couldn't place where from, who said he used to live abroad in the Middle East. Sitting on the back seat was a man who looked around 50 years old, wearing a suit jacket. He was from one of the neighbouring countries to Somalia.

The bus driver was a big bearded, toothless man wearing a turban. He was driving the bus fast and in a dangerous manner, causing peoples luggage to fall down from the compartments, making some passengers afraid and making them shout at him to slow down but he accelerated even more. A man was sitting two rows ahead with a young teenage girl who he was holding tightly as she sometimes screamed, kicking people, and banging her head against the ceiling of the bus. The father said, "She is mentally unwell and I took her to a traditional healer in Borama, Awdal province for treatment. She was responding well to the treatment in the early days, but she is back with the same behaviour." He started to hit her on the face and head.

The foreign man started shouting at somebody in the front of the bus in a very rude manner. Then, one of the comedy actors got up and told the driver, "Give me a rope to tight up the crazy girl's arms and legs like we do to the male camels." The driver said he would stop at the next town and get one.

Mr Solution, who was observing all this drama from the back seat of the bus, decided to bring some order to this bus journey as it appeared to be a crazy pantomime with a serious accident waiting to happen very soon.

Firstly, he told the father with the sick daughter to stop hitting her as it was making it even worse, but to give her cold water to drink then pour it over her head to cool her down and to communicate with her with love and affection instead of violence. The sick girl looked at Mr Solution with a dead-looking eye and a sweaty face from all the fighting and calmed down when the water was poured over her head. The father said, "Maybe you are a traditional healer with a blessed spirit as she has responded to your suggestion." Mr Solution laughed and said, "I don't think so, but if I opened a treatment centre like these religious traditional healers, I am sure I would make more money than them."

Then he moved the standing comedians back to their seat and told them, "This is not like your wacky comedy sketches or an animal, but a sick young lady", then he moved on to the foreign man and told him, "Remember, you're a guest in Somalia who probably does not have a valid visa, and this is not your country, so show respect to these people or you might get yourself in serious trouble." The man kept quiet and nodded. Then, Mr Solution approached the driver and said, "I think you have forgotten that this is not your personal car, but a company bus which I happened to help create with my idea, giving people like you jobs. You are transporting many people and are responsible for their safety and wellbeing, so drive like a professional." Then finally, he returned to his seat at the very back of the bus.

The rest of the journey was smooth without the drama and noise, stopping along the way to pick up and drop off passengers. The bus stopped for about 15 minutes at the bottom of the Sheikh Mountains, in a small village with a restaurant, a little mosque and shop specifically created for the passengers. The bus driver and his assistant, who were given free meals and drinks, always brought the travelling passengers in to rest, shop, eat and buy fresh fruits from the local farmers standing by the side of the road.

Mr Solution got off the bus, sat on a rock looking at the marvellous views of the surrounding mountains with lush green trees around and thought, 'I could really live here one day and be happy in this tranquil-looking place.' He also thought about how that idea given to businessmen to create a bus company travelling between the provinces of the country was making journeys cheaper and safer for the public and making integration possible.

It had indirectly changed things economically, creating jobs for millions of other people, and although Mr Solution was not profiting from this personally, it gave him great joy to see what could happen when genuine ideas and plans were created to help the citizens.

The bus was ready to leave and continue its journey again, honking its horn for passengers to board, when the suited foreign man grabbed his small bag and got off the bus, disappearing into the trees in the middle of this village, closely followed by the young slim man. Mr Solution thought it was unusual but chose to ignore it, arriving back safely in Burao at a good time of around 8 pm and reaching his home half an hour later.

He had an early night as Mr Solution was scheduled to travel the following day with a different bus company which travels at night time, only using minibuses, coming from Hargeisa to Garowe stopping via Burao to collect him as arranged by Mr Solution previously while he was there purchasing the plane tickets.

The following day, Mr Solution phoned the night minibus driver to Garowe and instructed him not to forget to save a seat in the front for him and to collect him from the petrol station. He then went to his regular coffee shop for his usual macchiato hit, followed by lunch and a chewing session with some local authority officers in a mansion on the outskirts of town to pass the time, watching live premiership football on the T.V until the bus arrived, as it was scheduled to pass through the pickup location around 10 pm.

There were around ten men and the odd female visitor from the neighbourhood in this house, including a kaban-playing musician and a folklore singer. The ten men comprised of two land hustlers called geometers, working for the provincial authorities, who measured land for people who wanted to purchase it for private or business use, with endless corrupt deals always causing land disputes and sometimes violent confrontations, three local residents who often arrived for the sessions, one person who was a former politician here but was still quite active working for the authorities, two were the sons of local import & export businessmen who spent their daddies' money causing mischief as they always got bailed out, and the musicians, who played and sang most of the afternoon while everyone joined in like a rowdy karaoke.

Most of the day was usually spent talking about local and regional politics, and joking about clan issues. Mr Solution said, "Don't you guys get tired of always talking about things which have happened in the past? Yesterday is gone, boys. Move on; we should be discussing today, tomorrow and the day after, which we can plan for and influence."

Mr solution understood the gentlemen enjoyed his company and stories of interesting adventures he had, but he also knew that some hated him because of his political views or his healthy, non-biased understanding of clan dynamics and the wider issues faced by people and country, so, as the guitar player stopped playing, one said, " Mr Solution, tell us what your plans are for tomorrow then." "Well, I am planning to catch a ride to Garowe either tonight or tomorrow and pass Tukaraq where this conflict everyone is talking about is, on a peace-making mission to silence the guns and move the fighting armies far apart."

The guy asking the question laughed and said, "That's the elders' and political leaders' job and if they can't sort it out, who do you think you are, little man?" Mr Solution laughed and said, "I did not get this nickname for no reason, Mister, and the difference between me and them, including you, is they talk about it but do nothing. I just do things simply and it gets the job done. I guess I have the touch for it; maybe it's mystical, but it's the genuine healthy approach I have".

Some cheers went up and the guitar man started to play again before this man said, "Since you're going, we shall soon see then". "Hopefully. I am only going to be away for no more than 5 days, so look forward to catching up again here on my return. Wish me well".

Around 9:30 pm, people were leaving to go home or continue their highs somewhere else.

Mr Solution was given a lift by one of the guys who was the son of a local businessman. Mr Solution said, "Drop me off at the petrol station on the main road out of the town. I have a bus coming to pick me up there soon." He sat chatting in the car to this guy who was trying his best to discourage Mr Solution from making the journey, saying "It's dangerous due to the tribe of the region who dislike our tribe because of our support for this administration here. Plus, the military is there fighting the other regional administration. It is the job of the politicians to sort this out, not yours."

"Thanks for the advice but I am different and know how to take care of himself in fast-moving situations."

He got out of the vehicle with leather travelling bag over his shoulder and entered the petrol station to buy a large bottle of Saxansaxo and some peanuts for the journey ahead. The shopkeeper said, "If you travelling out, there is a bus coming in 5 minutes. All the buses use us here. Shall I tell him there is a passenger ready and waiting?" "Normally, I would, but you know the proverb which says a man who does not keep a promise is one without faith? I have arrangements with another bus arriving in 30 minutes, booked days earlier who says he has been delayed a little, but thanks."

He crossed the road to a tea shop. It was now 11:30 pm and the driver kept saying he had passed this town and that town and wouldn't be much longer and for me to order him tea in a takeaway cup. Finally, after waiting hours, the minibus arrived around 1.45 am. The driver was acting suspicious as Mr Solution handed him the now cold tea he had asked for earlier.

As he went to use the toilet, a man with a southern Somalia accent, who was wearing shorts and appeared to be from the USA or Canada as he spoke English, came over to Mr Solution wanting a cigarette, introducing himself and saying he was on holiday and landed in Hargeisa and was now on his way to visit family in Galka'ayo, Mudug province. Then, as the driver returned, a little short man wearing traditional Arabic dress ran over with a little plastic bag, saying he was the passenger who made the booking and jumped on the bus. The driver said the bus was full and he could not take any more passengers,

Mr Solution said, "I don't know what's happening here, but I purposely did not board the other buses as I have been waiting for you, just as we planned days ago. Are you serious or overdosed on the khat tonight? Listen, man, we are skinny Somalis, apart from the ladies in the front there; I am sure I can squeeze in at the back." The passengers agreed, saying, "He can sit with us, no problem." However, the driver jumped into the bus and quickly droves away.

A small white Toyota with tinted windows came out of the petrol station. The driver smirked and said, "I guess there are no more buses coming tonight. Go home, man," then skidded his tyres and drove away. It was now approaching 2.30 am and there were no more buses coming until 7.30 am.

Mr Solution had just realised, after thinking about it, that this was all planned by individuals who did not want him to catch that bus, or to do what he had to do, but this incident made him even more determined to make the journey, however possible. He decided to wait around until the morning buses arrived, passing the time by sitting with a security guard at the petrol station and giving him plenty of potent Khat to stay alert and up until morning. He also provided him with hot tea as he had a flask nearby.

After a night of chewing and drinking plenty of caffeine, the morning buses started to arrive. The first one was the East to West 50-seater, but it was heading to another province called Sanaag, turning off the main road around 90 kilometres down the line. Mr Solution boarded it and planned to get off in a small village, just before it turned off, to catch another little minibus heading the way he wanted.

This bus was almost full, making its first journey, coincidently, since work had begun on a new 360-kilometres road which was around 70% complete.

Previously, only four by four cars could make the trip due to road conditions. He boarded the bus and paid $5. Most of the passengers said they were travelling from Hargeisa.

There was a woman who knew Mr Solution but was pretending she did not, asking questions like, "Is it your first time to Erigavo? I think you would like it." The bus briefly stopped at a garage to jack the tyres up with extra shocks for the suspension as they would be climbing some rough roads for part of the way as the roadworks were slow but continuing. Mr Solution replied, "If I was travelling there, it would be my first time. I hear it has beautiful scenery for tourists to explore, such as the Daallo mountains, beaches, waterfalls and rich agricultural lands." The lady, who now had a young boy sitting next to her, all of a sudden said, "Why not? You should come with us as there have been bloody re-occurring tribal killings in a district of the province and since you are Mr Solution, you can mediate, right?"

"How do you know my nickname?" Realising she had made a mistake by the reaction on her face, she replied, "I thought you just told me." "No, I did not, so what's your name, lady?" She gave a fake name as the kid sitting next to her looked on, shocked.

Mr Solution realised that she and others on the bus knew of the work he had done previously and they were also aware of the trip he was making today to bring peace to a military conflict which could explode any time into all-out war, but they wished to divert him to a different place to help solve a tribal conflict there, so after a 45-minute journey on the bus, Mr solution got off the bus in the little village where the two roads separate to wait and catch his minibus heading straight on to Garowe via Tukaraq.

With his bag over his shoulder, in a little dusty village with a few people, goats and chickens running around, Mr Solution went to a little hut to take shade and get hot tea while waiting for the minibus as he was feeling hot and tired due to lack of sleep. The tea man arrived and said, "The pot is boiling so it won't be long." A few other villagers arrived to see the new arrival and there were the usual exchanges of news for the day, like how the water resources and pastures were for livestock around the villages, Mr Solution says to the tea man, "Tea all round for the men here too, please. When is the next bus arriving heading towards Garowe?"

One of the men from the village said, "They should be rolling up soon, all day until mid-afternoon. You can wait here or from back there at the security stop where there is a policeman in a little hut."

After drinking his tea, followed by some small talk regarding how their environment was, and with them finding it difficult to gather any more information about him, an old lady they call the auntie of the village emerged from behind the tea hut. Mr Solution said, "Get a fresh pot of tea made for the auntie as well." The tea was delivered to the auntie, who was sitting in a traditional chair called a gambadh in the one-room home behind. Mr Solution greeted her and had a brief chat just like the rest before she asked about the journey and his tribe identification and Mr Solution said the same thing - "I am from the Somali tribe, auntie, just like you; goodbye."

Then he went to the checkpoint where all cars stop for the police officer to remove the barrier on the road, bought some fresh camel milk in a reused water bottle from a tin shack of a shop, then sat on a rock underneath a tree for some shade from the sun.

A woman came over after 20 minutes then crossed over to the other side of the road where the police hut was. She sat underneath a tree for shade. Mr Solution came over and offered her a bottle of water as it was a hot day, then the policeman invited Mr Solution to his little hut to sit until the bus arrived, but, little did Mr Solution know, a drama and an abduction were about to follow.

The police officer was an old man with broken thick glasses on. Next to his hut was a weird-looking imported caravan, which appeared completely out of place in this little village in the middle of nowhere. He explained that it was used as a prison cell to hold people.

Several minibuses came past the checkpoint, but all the bus drivers said they were full, although, Mr Solution could see clearly that they had spaces available. It seemed strange to Mr Solution for them to turn down good money unless they had been paid a lot to comply.

The policeman kept receiving plenty of expensive khat to chew along with drinks and cigarettes from passing cars on both sides of the road, which was also abnormal, as generally, the policemen at the barriers were disliked by drivers but Mr Solution thought nothing of it at that stage. The policeman kept saying, "I have a bus which will take you and he is coming soon. Don't worry, chew this khat and relax."

Some little schoolgirls came over for some drinking water and the policeman was having inappropriate conversations with the children. It was now almost 1 pm. Mr Solution was hot and bothered and said to the policeman, "Sit down, you dirty old man. Stop talking to the children like that before I make you sit with your old rifle, if it works; maybe I should test it right now." the policeman started to choke on the green stuff he had been chewing and said, "Go, girls, I am just kidding. Stop playing, Mister - I am gonna sit."

Mr Solution put the gun back in its place when he sat, but for a moment, due to lack of sleep and proper food, not to mention all the chewing of that khat stuff, he was prepared to fire the gun and shoot this terrible old man, but thank God that did not happen. He thought, 'That would have made my hands dirty and that's not my style.'

The large trucks working for the road development agency building the new road were turning off near the village. As they drove past, the drivers were covering their face so Mr Solution did not see who was driving. It was a very unusual thing to do, although Mr Solution, who had made all this possible as it was his idea and plan in the first place, knew individuals, who had been giving jobs in the project, were often used by the authorities to conduct errands outside of their remit.

Mr Solution went to pray at midday prayers and cool down spiritually and clean himself with cold water from the water container behind the hut. As he finished, a white Toyota estate car pulled up and three men got out and said, "Get in the car; we are leaving." The three men were familiar to Mr Solution. Two were cousins and the other was a relative who had recently been made a tribal chief without the consent or the traditional process, due to political reasons as wanted by the regional regime, who are heavily influenced if not controlled by these groups who use extreme religious ideology to obtain money and power to dominate the population and one of their strategies had been recently to take over the leadership of tribes by funding and selecting fake tribal chiefs.

Mr Solution said, "I'm surprised to see you here wanting to go to Garowe. Last I remembered, you were attempting to discourage me from going due to your alliances." Two more men with shoddy-looking police uniforms also arrived, and by this time, Mr Solution was surrounded.

The tribal chief said, "We are taking you back to Burao with us," then Mr Solution was physically handled by all and bundled into the car by force. He was being held in the back seat by two men on either side holding his hands, one holding a rope, wanting to tie his hands together, then one of the men grappled Mr Solution in a headlock, also trying to damage his left eye with a thump. Mr Solution was in pain and finding it difficult to breathe, so, he bit a chunk out of the man's arm with his teeth.

Mr Solution said, "I will comply and go back with you. Look, I am already in the car, so calm down and sit properly and give me some space and let's enjoy the drive back." The situation calmed down, then, around an hour later, they arrived back in Burao. Stopping near the tribal meeting house, Mr Solution said to the abductors, "Goodbye. You have done the job of bringing me back, as ordered by your masters, now leave." He got out of the car, slamming the door on the way out.

Although it had been almost two days since he had slept, Mr Solution decided to go to the shack café opposite for a plate of pasta with sauce and continue chewing khat to plan how he should make his journey to Garowe.

It was now late in the evening. Mr Solution made a call to a new minibus company called Sahan, meaning explore in the city, to find out departure times and make a booking for two days' time by paying in advance. Once this booking was done Mr Solution was more relaxed as he knew another attempt to make the journey had been scheduled rapidly.

There is a proverb which says "if one wants to go fast then go alone; if one wants to travel the longest distance then take a companion". Because of the things Mr Solution wanted to solve, it required him to move alone on this mission.

Once this booking was confirmed, Mr Solution decided to go to his home to get some much-needed sleep and rest for the following day as he would attempt to travel again, unless more obstacles appeared.

That morning, he hit the town, meeting a few people to make them aware he would be travelling to Garowe via Tukaraq for business and personal reasons and for them to make sure he did not face any problems like before by neutralising any issues on his way out of the city and throughout the journey up to Aynaba town, close to Las Anod, where they had leverage. After that, Mr Solution would be able to handle matters as the local people would grant him an uninterrupted journey because of connections there, such as some Garaads of the region.

He arrived at the bus company's offices located in the central east side of town. The passengers had not all arrived yet, so he spoke with the office agent, and informed him that he had already paid for a ticket the day before, showing the reference details. He said, "I know who you are. You will be travelling on bus number 302, which is outside being loaded by the driver, but you are early. It is scheduled to leave in one hour and forty-five minutes' time. Here is your bus ticket." Mr Solution thanked the agent, noticing his accent was from a different province than this region, and stepped outside to meet the driver. "Driver, I will be one of your passengers. Keep the front seat empty for me. I am going to get some breakfast; would you like me to get you something?" "Just a cup of tea, please, and don't be late."

He made the short walk round the corner to a back-alley restaurant serving traditional breakfast and ordered the pan-fried fresh camel liver with vegetables, served with Lahooh/ Anjeelo (a type of sourdough bread) with a Somali-style tea to wash it down. After eating breakfast slowly to kill some time, he approached the counter to pay and ordered tea with a little snack as a takeaway for the driver. Sitting in the corner were two guys whose faces were familiar, pretending not to see Mr Solution, who walked over as he was exiting the restaurant and said, "Boys, I hope you have learned your lessons; not today!"

Then, he walked towards the bus offices where nearly all the passengers were boarding the bus. The driver was on top of the bus loading the passengers' bags. "Driver, I have your tea," he said. "Sit on the front seat reserved for you; I will be down shortly."

Mr Solution boarded, looking quickly at the passengers with his shades on, checking the types of people on board. They were a mixture of men and women. The driver came down, started the engine and said to the passengers "Come off, please. Wait for 5 minutes while I check my tyre pressure levels from the shop, then come past the local police station to get clearance to leave."

The passengers got off. Mr Solution sat on the steps of the office to smoke a cigarette, along with another passenger travelling to a different location who had a middle provinces accent, until the driver returned; he took longer than the anticipated five minutes he said, however, he returned after a while and all the passengers boarded the bus again.

"Driver, here is your tea and a little snack to have with it. Good job, by the way." He smiled, took the tea and played the Mp3 player with jazzy soulful driving music.

The driver was 25 years old and said he was from Las Anod, which is the provincial capital of Sool, the province where this conflict standoff between two rival administrations military was taking place. "How often do you make this journey, driver?" "Every two days I drive between Burao, Togdheer and Garowe," he replied. He was driving fast, not stopping for hitch-hikers or entertaining police stops along the way. This gave Mr Solution the confidence that the driver could be trusted to get him to his destination safely, on time and could even be of assistance.

Around 10:30 am, the new Toyota minibus passed the police checkpoint where Mr Solution had been kidnapped and returned to Burao some days before. "Goodbye, you horrible little village," said Mr Solution out of the window of the bus. The driver looked over with a smile and said, "You don't like this village; did you have some trouble here before? Don't worry, you are with us now, in my province." Mr Solution smiled and said, "Good to know you. Boys from Sool understand the situation; you must be part of the help, so let's stop at the next town and I will get us some chew chew for the rest of the journey."

The bus stopped at Aynaba town for ten minutes. Some passengers got off there as it was the end of their journey, while others went to the shops or toilets to relieve themselves. Mr Solution went to a khat dealer to purchase a small amount for the driver and himself. The passengers boarded again and the journey continued to Las Anod to stop for lunch. A passenger at the back is giving a guided tour of important historical locations of past events, such as where military battles happened between Somali independence fighter, Zayid Abdullah Hassan, also known as the mad mullah, and by the British who fought a bloody conflict with his army called the Darwiishs for 21 years against the British from the end of the 18 century to the 1920s.

Around 1.45 pm, the minibus arrived at their office in Las Anod city centre for passengers alighting there to get off, while others and parcels were loaded to continue to its final destination of Garowe. The driver told the passengers to wait outside the offices while he went to a garage to check up on the bus and pass through the local police station for clearance.

Mr Solution took a walk to a hotel and restaurant in the middle of town for some refreshments. The hotel was owned by somebody known to Mr Solution who would be able to inform him about the matters within the province, including the conflict further ahead in Tukeraq. While there, Mr Solution, in a loud manner so all can hear, told a group of people sitting around a table, "I don't think it's just me who understands this Tukeraq is a compound of two words meaning crow eats! And if I am not wrong, the crow eats dead meat, only it does not hunt living things by itself, so therefore, it sounds like this conflict in your province will give plenty of dead human meat to the crows in Tukeraq and if I am not wrong, the majority of dead human meat on both sides of the conflict will be of the people of Sool, so the right thing to do is refuse to fight over something which has no real value. Personally, I like a good fight, but only if it's a must of high value; don't allow the military to conduct a war over your children's heads and, if you must raise a flag, let it be the national flag, not these local regional ones."

There was complete silence from the audience. Mr Solution then left the hotel restaurant and went back to the bus offices to continue the journey, buying fresh camel milk from an old lady sitting outside on the side of the road, sharing a joke; "Las Anod means the borehole of milk in our language, so give me one more bottle, mama, for the driver please." He arrived back at the bus offices and everybody was on board. the only person missing was Mr Solution. "Sorry, driver, went to get some milk from your city. I got a bottle for you too, since you are named the city of milk. I hope the peace follows it soon."

Mr Solution knew he had just delivered a powerful speech to the people there, telling them the truth in an informal relaxed way, which others were afraid to say or purposely did not because of political interests of the war-makers on either side. This sort of speech would reach it's intended target very quickly and they would have to act immediately as the truth was sometimes bitter, but would liberate you in the end.

They continued the journey, passing the wreckage of a plane from Kenya, which had crashed by the side of the road, as it had run out of fuel on approach to the airport. Then, around thirty minutes later, they reached the village of Tukeraq, with men wearing military uniform and heavy guns sitting around in groups outside these tea and khat shops, then, after the line of control, further on were a bunch of pickup trucks armed with artillery guns with soldiers sitting under the shade of the trees. The driver was explaining who the different militias and military groups were.

They stopped to pick up four men in military uniform from the Puntland side of the conflict, who wanted to go to Garowe. Mr Solution got off the bus to allow the men to board, giving them cigarettes as he lit one while another traveller went to urinate in the bushes nearby.

One of the soldiers sat next to Mr Solution and said, "Real men do not hurt each other over worthless things." This gave an indication to Mr Solution that these men had heard what was said earlier in Las Anod.

Mr Solution smiled and said, "You are right, general, and know, it isn't the sons of either side's regional leaders who will die in this conflict, but some poor dad's son dying in a worthless conflict. We are not stupid; here, have some of this chew chew with me; we all should tell the military leaders of both sides to move back which will create space so this unnecessary conflict can settle down."

Mr Solution heard other passengers agreeing by nodding their heads or saying that it was the right thing to do.

The driver put his sunglasses on and played a particular classic Somali song, which Mr Solution likes very much, called "shimbiryahow ma duusha, ma dabeylo raacda, dadka ma u adeegta oo ma u dada'shaa, dimnaha kala qaad oo dal yaqaan ma tahay degmodii fogaatiyo dawgeeda ma garata". This translates as, "bird, do you fly, do you go with the wind, do you serve the people, open your lips, do you know the country, can you locate a distant district?" This was by Magool, a celebrated singer like the Aretha Franklin of soul music. This song has a message of positive poetic lyrics, and the volume was turned up by Mr Solution as he felt the song was talking to him in a way.

The bus arrived in Garowe, its final destination, around 4 pm. This town, which is the regional administrations capital, is a fairly new town created within the last 20 years in a flat landscape, measuring around only 10 kilometres square, with an estimated population of 150,000 people at best.

Mr Solution asked the driver if he knew a decent hotel, and the driver said, "Yes, I will take you to a hotel with a good location where I stay sometimes." The town was busy with lots of people visiting from various provinces, as a hotly contested regional election was scheduled within the coming weeks between the current regional incumbent leader, who was a former prime minister of Somalia and at least ten others. After a short drive around the town, dropping off passengers, the bus parked outside a three-floor hotel called Janteela, which had a busy restaurant and cafeteria outside.

Approaching the hotel counter, he asked for two single rooms. The man said, "I only have a shared family room with three beds as we are fully booked up due to all the visitors for the elections, but as soon as a single room becomes available, I will inform you." Since it was a fair explanation, Mr Solution said, "We will take it." The room was located on the top floor next to a flat rooftop with benches and tables for guests to relax, drink and watch the view of the town all round. For a moment, Mr Solution thought he had been given the penthouse room.

The small bag carried by Mr Solution and the driver's plastic one were stored in the basic room then they returned to the hotel courtyard inside to order some much-needed food from the good selection on offer. Mr Solution ordered the steak with Muufo bread and a large fresh watermelon juice. After the food, the driver said he would visit his local office and Mr Solution went outside to sit with the locals drinking tea, checking the atmosphere of the people. Most of them were tribal leaders, dressed in colourful traditional dresses, who were tasked with selecting the people's representatives who would then elect the regional leader. There were election organisers, candidate campaigners, current local officials, political brokers, and other hustlers, such as moving traders who were selling goods as there was lots of money circulating during this time which was good for all independent traders.

Mr Solution made sure the small traders selling goods to feed their family were empowered economically by always purchasing stuff from them when the opportunity arose, so when a man carrying a variety of items for sale on his shoulder and hands passed by near the cafeteria, Mr Solution noticed the African-style handmade hats he had on him. "Hey, Mister, bring those hats over, please." The man brought them over and said, "It's only 15 dollars." Mr Solution placed one on his head and took a picture on his mobile phone to view it and, surprisingly, it looked really good on him so he said, "Very nice; I look like dhaqe sare!" meaning the top cultivator if translated directly. "Thanks. Here is 20 dollars - I think it's worth it."

Then, all of a sudden, there was a frenzy of buyers from all the customers sitting around the cafeteria, purchasing at least 5 other hats, so the trader was extremely happy with his day's trading activity. The waiter came out telling him he had to leave. "We pay taxes, you don't; this is a restaurant and, Mr High Hat, stop encouraging the hawkers." He was pointing at Mr Solution who responded, "I am not the only High Hat-wearing person here; look around." He turned to look around and saw many were wearing the high hats purchased from the mobile trader and there was complete laughter at the waiter who returned to the kitchen with his tray, looking slightly embarrassed.

Mr Solution got his phone out and wrote the blunt message he had delivered in Las Anod on his social media and political party pages, also informing some key collaborators that he had arrived in Garowe on a mission, knowing they would also travel by air or road here to get involved in the elections.

Mr Solution noticed some people such as militiamen and tribal chiefs from the Buuhoodle district of Togdheer province, who were part of this administration only because they support the unity of the country; he called over the waiter and said, "Give their table whatever they are drinking or eating then put it on my hotel bill". They didn't know who he was or where Mr Solution was from, but a military-style salute was made by one of the men sitting at their table as the orders rolled in.

Mr Solution did not know it then, but the chairman of the election was sitting close by. He was a regular of the hotel and restaurant, who thought maybe this young gentleman wanted to be part of this new election and the government being constructed. He would be a very interesting candidate which would make headlines due to his tribe, however, Mr Solution was not there for the election and had specifically travelled here on a peace-keeping mission and to get a new Somali passport then return to Burao unless some resourceful people travelled over from Mogadishu to take him there.

It was late in the evening. The sun was setting. After dinner and drinks, Mr Solution entered the hotel restaurant to pay his bills for the day. A large woman was sitting at the cashier's desk and said, "How do you want to pay?" "Cash please," and a one hundred US dollar bill was handed to her. The lady said, "I don't have the change in paper money but can send it to your mobile wallet or you can go to the money-changer man across the road by the bus stop." Mr Solution left the building to get it changed by this man, who had a box full of local and international currencies, sitting under an umbrella by the bus stop. He could change the currency into smaller denominations for a fee.

The money exchange man noticed Mr Solution was not a local man but had travelled in, so he said, "If you need any other services such as arrangements making a passport application or further foreign exchange, call me on this number," and he handed him a piece of paper with the money.

Mr Solution thanked him then returned to the woman at the hotel, who was making enquiries about where he had travelled from. "I am from Burao, Togdheer, and which province do you come from, lady?" "I come from Hargeisa originally, but have lived here for a long time as my husband and children are from this province." She attempted to ascertain the tribal group of Mr Solution, without success, before he returned to his hotel room to relax for the rest of the evening. Mr Solution was suspicious of this woman as she could have been an informer to Hargeisa who were regularly snooping and trying to find out the purpose of one's visit.

The driver returned late in the evening to also rest in one of the available beds in the shared family room. An early start was planned by all; morning breakfast in the hotel courtyard then an appointment with a local man who would be driving and showing Mr Solution around the offices of the local administration, such as the district offices, registration building, police station, and taking pictures to obtain certain documents for the passport application.

Outside, the money exchange man was phoned and then a call was made to his friend the driver, who arrived ten minutes later to pick up Mr Solution. Mr Solution already had six passport-sized pictures so he directed him to the registrar's office, where there was a long queue of people all wanting the same documents.

The driver, whose job it was to make this process quick and simple, contacted one of his colleagues who worked there. Documents and information were handed over to him then they went to the district offices building to pay some more fees to the local Puntland authority to obtain further information needed for the application. The queue for this building was even longer. Most of the people had travelled a long distance, some almost 700 kilometres, some of the people were extremely sick children who needed urgent passports to travel abroad for treatment such as kidney replacements. One little boy who had travelled from Burao explained, "Both my kidneys don't function, so, twice a week, I attend Burao General Hospital for dialysis treatment on a new machine just installed, so we need to return as soon as we finish with the passport application today, or at the latest, tomorrow." There were patients needing complicated surgery, so Mr Solution talked with the officials and queuing people to allow them quick access due to their health situations. Inside the district offices, he said very loudly so all could hear, "It is a bad political decision by those leaders over there; the people from northern Somalia have to travel a long distance, pay for hotels, travel costs for what they are rightfully entitled to in their own cities but denied by their so-called authority. It makes no sense; you have to demand changes, people, so a passport office can be opened in places like Burao which is a province central to all the northern territories."

A very attractive young lady, who had the unusual name of Ashqarar, approached Mr Solution and said, "Yes, yes; can you talk to them to make this happen?" Mr Solution replied, "It's a team effort; I will do my part but you all need to do your bit".

An appointment for the following day was made with the office staff before leaving and heading to the town centre for mid-day prayer and sightseeing. The driver was released for the day as Mr Solution had decided to go for a walk instead, as it was a fairly small town. Outside the district offices was a young gentleman whom Mr Solution had recruited to his people's party of Somalia when they met in a ceremony organised by the national youth organisation in Mogadishu six years earlier. He was born in a district town called Buhoodle, part of the Togdheer province but politically not part of it. This gentleman and his team were transferred to the current Somali president's political campaign some years earlier by Mr Solution to get him elected as he was the best of the candidates at the time, resulting in him being successful.

In a brief chat, he said he had arrived a week ago and had been selected as a candidate to be part of the new regional parliament; he appeared a little chubby compared to how Mr Solution remembered him.

Contact details were exchanged and he said, "Some of the other young men you met years earlier in Mogadishu are scheduled to arrive tomorrow by plane. I will give them your mobile number as I am sure you're cooking up something here as usual!" Mr Solution smiled and said, "Please do; they would be helpful as most of them were from Las Anod if I remember correctly. I am here on a peace-keeping mission to do my part in stopping the conflict in Tukeraq between these two rivals and to get a Somali passport made before I return to Europe." He asked, "Have you not been back to Europe since 2012?" "No, man, I have been in Africa the entire time; more than 6 years now. Can't you tell? I look like one of the locals!"

He headed to the town centre, surprised at how clean this town was. No litter anywhere. While buying cigarettes, he asked a local shopkeeper, "Is it always this clean in the town?" He laughed and said, "Because of the elections and visitors, the local authority is putting on a show by actually doing some work for once." He continued the walk around town to a mosque to pray. This particular mosque was said to be the oldest in the town and its imam and the majority of worshippers were from the traditional Somali Muslim Sufi groups. Prayer is performed then they left the building as usual. Mr Solution did not belong to any particular group so, to him, mosques were all houses of God, all facing the same direction towards Mecca, so he prayed in the nearest one when the time of prayer approached. This had baffled some groups who wanted to recruit him to their sects, but as he did not identify with any of them, apart from being a Somali Muslim, he was not restricted to any certain mosques.

The restaurants in town didn't look too appetising, so Mr Solution walked back to the hotel restaurant where lunch was ready to be served to hotel guests and the general public. The bus driver had also returned and said, "I have already eaten my lunch. When you finish eating your food, let's meet outside by the minibus because we are going for a drive."

Mr Solution agreed and ordered his lunch with a cold glass of papaya and passion fruit juice to drink with it. As the food and drink arrived, he noticed a man sitting at the corner table alone, quietly, appearing fed up. Mr Solution felt uncomfortable eating unless the status of this man's lunch was known, so he called the waiter over and told him to find out if that man had eaten lunch, and if not, to take his order and put it on his bill.

The waiter asked the man who says he is from another province called Mudug looking for relatives and has not eaten all day. Then the waiter takes his order; he only orders a plate of rice, but the waiter says, "Order whatever you like. That man waiting to eat his food will pay for it all." He replied, "Very kind of him. May God bless and grant all his wishes. Give me the same as he is having, please," pointing at Mr Solution who now feels like he can enjoy his lunch comfortably. When he was finished, he waited outside leaning on the minibus smoking a cigarette when the driver arrived and said, "I am going to show you where the regional president's house and government buildings such as the Immigration and passport office are located."

It was early afternoon when they hopped on the minibus and within 10 minutes, the bus reached the corner of the town on a newly built road with big compounds belonging to the regional administrations, the United Nations, several NGO organisations including the national death foundation and the nationality and immigration building where Mr Solution planned to be the following day once all the remaining paperwork was completed.

After an hour's drive around the small town, they returned to the hotel and checked in with the hotel reception to collect the room key. The receptionist was away to the restaurant so the hotel manager fetched the keys and as Mr Solution and the driver were leaving, he said, "There will be two new guests in your room tonight, also from Burao, so I will have to ask the bus driver to make the room available." Mr Solution did not like the idea of sharing a room with strangers as he would have to sleep with one eye open, so he said to the hotel manager, "I requested a single room initially, that's what I am paying for, so please inform me as soon as one becomes vacant".

Late in the evening, two young men knocked on the room door saying they would be staying in this room for a few days as they needed an urgent national passport to travel abroad to continue their further education and had just come off the bus from Burao. This seemed like a plausible reason to Mr Solution, so he said, "Those two beds are available; put your bags down there. The toilets and showers are just outside the room on the right near the roof garden." One of the young men introduced himself, saying he knew who Mr Solution was by clan identifications and residence in Burao.

Instantly, he became even more alert to their presence as he suspected they were two young boys paid then sent from Burao by the individuals who were making travel here difficult, with many obstacles along the way, to spy on the activities of Mr Solution and God knows what else.

After a sleepless night due to the new guests, Mr Solution woke up very early then phoned the man tasked with making the arrangements for the remaining documents to complete the passport application that day. The man arrived promptly to drive him to the local central police station for the certification. Outside the registry office, a policeman is guarding the front entrance of the building. He befriends Mr Solution by suggesting he gets some breakfast as the paperwork will not be ready until after midday, so he gets another officer to replace him. He takes him to a Yemeni restaurant nearby, opened by refugees from Yemen living in Somalia due to the war in their country. The officer ordered a large plateful of chickpeas, roasted vegetables and eggs with a large flatbread.

"Do you see that man and the woman bending over peeling the onions in the bucket? They are dirty, filthy individuals! Do you know I caught them in the kitchen one late night performing nasty sexual acts considered forbidden in Somalia; I arrested them then freed them as I was embarrassed to note down the reasons for their arrest, but instead, I get free food whenever I am here so you don't have to pay for the breakfast." Feeling uncomfortable with this information, Mr Solution got up, washed his hands then paid for the breakfast with a five-dollar note, telling the waiter to keep the change. He rushed out of the restaurant to return to the registry office.

Then finally, late in the evening, he got to the passport office to request a fast-tracked passport within seven days by paying an extra service fee. The foreign exchange man, who had been given the cost of all the fees, sent the payment to the immigration official's payment account and said, "You can now go back to Burao on the bus which is leaving shortly. I can collect the passport and send it on the bus for you if you leave the receipt with me to give authorisation." Mr Solution declined the offer. "Thanks, but no thanks. I will keep the receipt and collect it on another occasion and will not be travelling back today as I have a few more things to do here in Garowe."

After a long day spent travelling from place to place, he returned to the hotel in the evening to shower and freshen up for an evening out in the good company of some fine ladies he had met earlier outside the passport office, who said they lived in a villa rented by the UN as one of the girls worked for them.

As Mr Solution was leaving, the two young men from Burao entered the hotel reception. Mr Solution handed them the room key and asked, "What happened to you guys? I did not see you in any of the usual offices or the immigration department as scheduled." One of the lads replied, "We were delayed so we shall go early tomorrow morning instead." "Ok, leave the keys with the reception for me to collect as I may return very late."

Mr Solution spent most of the evening with these interesting girls and two local men who had returned from a holiday in Australia. They had been chewing the chew chew, while the girls drank orange soft drinks and ate traditional sweets while singing to music videos playing on the large T.V screen.

Early in the morning, Mr Solution returned to the hotel, after praying Fajr prayer in the local mosque, to wake up the young boys to go to their appointments as mentioned the previous day, and also, for Mr Solution to get a good deep sleep for the day while they were away.

It was hot and humid but he had a good day's rest, then late in the evening, the boys returned, informing him, "We are checking out to catch a bus leaving shortly back to Burao. Why don't you come back with us? There is space available." Mr Solution declined the offer but went downstairs to make sure the boys caught their return bus, and also to ask the hotel receptionist about the single room requested. He says that two rooms would be available tomorrow as the guests were scheduled to check out, but to remain in the same three-bed room for one more night.

Around midnight, there was a knock on the door. Mr Solution, who had been sleeping, woke up and asked who it was. A man said, "Open up!" Mr Solution opened the door. It was a large, bald, sweaty, charcoal-coloured man wearing a vest, who said that one of the beds had been rented to him by the hotel now as he was a bus driver who had just arrived from a place called Bosaso.

Mr Solution went downstairs to confirm with the hotel receptionist, but it was closed so he went back upstairs and told the new arrival, "Hey, man, there is no one in reception downstairs. How did you book yourself in?" The man replied, "I phoned him, but I was delayed due to a breakdown along the way. I can sleep outside on the rooftop." He then started to take the mattress and duvet outside and Mr Solution threw a pillow out to him. "No disrespect, but I was not expecting anybody at this late time."

First thing in the morning, before breakfast, Mr Solution went to the hotel manager in reception to collect the keys for the single room downstairs. The man informed him that the room was being cleaned and changed by the hotel maids, so should be ready after breakfast.

Mr Solution was not leaving until he sorted out this room which had become a problem causing him a loss of vital sleep, so he visited the restaurant for a double espresso while he waited. The gardener was in the courtyard watering plants. "Good morning. Have you worked here for a long time?" He said he had worked there for two years. "Is it normal for a hotel guest to arrive at 2 am? If so, who lets them in?" "Hey, Mister, I am just a gardener. The hotel receptionist or the security guard would know better, but many long-distance drivers bring customers here at various times and they get free accommodation as an agreement with the man inside.". He nodded at the gardener, then went back inside to hotel reception to collect the keys for the new room.

There he saw two super-heavy ladies coming out, who Mr Solution recognised as being part of the civil society members in Garowe as they were always shown on local T.V stations when political events or rallies were taking place. Being a gentleman, Mr Solution held the door open for the ladies to exit, then approached reception who finally had a new room ready. Mr Solution collected his belongings from the room upstairs, then went to the new ground-floor room which had two single beds.

Mr Solution returned to reception to hand the keys back. "I thought you said it was a single room. There are two beds." "Don't worry, it's a single room just for you," said the receptionist.

Mr Solution went to settle his restaurant bills before going out to do some shopping for the day. He paid the bills to the lady at the counter, who said, "Now you have concluded your passport application here, are you not returning today? there is a bus leaving in the afternoon." Mr Solution, who was enjoying the change of scenery from Burao, was getting the feeling somebody wanted him to go back ASAP and it was certainly not the local people of Garowe, so he said, "Not yet, good lady. I like Garowe; might even move here permanently." He started walking down the main road towards the town centre, visiting clothes shops first, looking for traditional stuff made locally but, unfortunately, he found that all the goods were imported from Asia, China or India mainly, which did not appeal to him. He wanted to purchase products made locally in order to support the growth of the national economy, and also create jobs for the country's citizens, as they were experiencing a major deficit in exports.

As lunchtime was approaching and the town was frantically busy with all the election campaigning, with enormous advertising boards with different candidate's faces and slogans springing up daily, Mr Solution went to a hotel in the centre, occupied by several candidates, to meet their campaigners for lunch and to get a feel of who looked favourite or a suitable candidate for the people.

There was a candidate the people were talking about as being different who could bring unity and success. He had just recently returned from the USA and was originally from the disputed Sool province where Mr Solution was working hard to stop any further conflict erupting between the two federal states wishing to control it fully. However, there was strong opposition from the current incumbent and other candidates. Also, the Somali land administration had sent funds to other candidates so he was not elected as they viewed him as a person who would take away all support in that province. Talking to some of his campaign guys over lunch, Mr Solution said, "Your man Mr Isse would be an ideal regional president for real change to shake things up, but unless you can convince these old tribal boys with the high hats to select your candidate, I think it will be a futile attempt".

A call was received from the Sahan bus driver who was supposed to drive back to Burao. He said that, unexpectedly, he had to stay for several more days before making the trip back to Burao. However, he had a driver leaving this afternoon. Should he book a seat for him? "No, but make a booking for me in the morning; pickup is outside the hotel," said Mr Solution, who returned to the hotel for the rest of the day to prepare for the following day's 6-hour drive back.

Morning came, and a new minibus from a company named Sky Blue stopped just outside the hotel. There was a chubby driver who said he was from Hargeisa, where this bus journey would terminate after dropping off and picking up passengers along the way. Mr Solution loaded his leather travel bag onto the roof of the bus, watching as it was loaded to make sure it was strapped tightly.

Mr Solution climbed on board and sat on the very back seat with two Ethiopians in the corner. One was a crippled man who used crutches to walk. The other was a quiet young man who did not have the usual Ethiopian facial features. There was also a young suited local man who said he was from Gaalka'ayo. In the middle section, there were at least four young mothers with their kids from the deep southern provinces of the country, judging by their accents. Two were travelling with their husbands, who were sitting just in front of them, and right at the front was a woman wearing all-black middle-eastern abaya-style clothing.

The minibus was all loaded up and ready to leave, stopping at a petrol station on the way out for some diesel and for passengers to purchase soft drinks.

The woman sitting at the front seat went into the petrol station to purchase something. As Mr Solution was sitting right at the back, it would require all the passengers in the middle section to get off to let him out, so, not to inconvenience them, he shouted at the woman, "My sister, here is the money; can you please get me a large bottle of water?" The woman turned around and walked towards the bus window. As she did so, Mr Solution noticed she was walking like those girls he used to remember in western countries, almost like a fashion event, cat-walk style. When she came over, Mr Solution handed over five dollars and said, "Biyo weyn," meaning large water, but she responded "aaa uu" as if she did not understand what he just said, so Mr Solution, who needed the water as he had started chewing khat for the journey ahead, said "Biyo, Biyo," with hand actions. She then smiled and said, "Haa," meaning yes. She turned around to enter the shop. Mr Solution watched her walk away and was amazed at her style of walking which would arouse the attention of any normal healthy male.

When she returned with the water and a handful of inflated Somali currency in her hand, Mr Solution noticed she had a curvy, tight and extremely physically fit-looking body under her black Islamic or Arabic-looking dress. When she handed over the water and his change, Mr Solution said, "Thanks, pretty lady." She smiled and said, in an American or Canadian accent, "mahadsan", meaning just thanks.

The bus drove on for about two hours before stopping at Las Anod police checkpoint, where passengers were checked. The two Ethiopians remained inside the bus, while all the other passengers got off. Mr Solution told the sitting men in military uniform, "There are two Ethiopian passengers inside. Are you not calling them out to be checked like all the Somali citizens you are checking inside their own country?" He just kept silent and told the driver to leave by lifting the metal barrier, so Mr Solution went to the bus and told the Ethiopian passengers to come out to be checked like everyone else, but the official refused, telling them to get back on board. His actions made the passengers concerned about the two Ethiopian men, particularly Mr Solution, who was sitting next to them at the back of the bus. This made him very alert for any unexpected reactions of the passengers.

Mr Solution was keen to speak with the girl in the black figure-hugging abaya dress and finally got the chance as the bus stopped at their office. He stopped at the toilet then went to a local shop to spend the handful of national currency buying sweets for the kids in the bus and a cold glass of camel milk for the lady in the black abaya dress, who was sitting in the corner alone outside the office. "Hey there, this is for you," he said, handing over the cold drink of milk. She tried to ask in Somali language what it was but was struggling, as she did not want to be recognised as a foreign person. So, Mr Solution said, "It is premium fresh cold camel's milk in English." She laughed and said, "My Aabo (meaning dad) says we should not drink it as it will give us uncontrollable runs, apparently, as I am not used to drinking it." Mr Solution asked, "Where did you come from and what's your name?"

"My name is Suleka. I am a Somali American. My Aabo is an old-fashioned African Somali man who brought us home as he said we needed to learn about our country and our cultural roots. My mother is an African American woman, so I am half-Somali, but don't tell that to my dad. He says we are just Somali and everything else second. I escaped from the rest of the family and I am travelling alone to Hargeisa to visit some friends from abroad and get some city vibes after being bored in villages and small towns for weeks." Mr Solution thought, for some reason, that maybe she was the daughter of the famous Somali supermodel and more recently businesswoman, Iman, also the wife of British rock star David Bowie, as she had a daughter with a former American baseball player, before Bowie, also named Suleikha, but then that might be simply a coincidence.

"How come you speak such fluent English? You are also from abroad, right?" Mr Solution replies "Yes, I am also a Somali returnee who travelled from the UK more than 6 years ago now. I am travelling to my home city of Burao along the way to Hargeisa." "How do you feel when you chew that green stuff in your mouth? Does it make you high?" "It's a different type of feeling high compared to alcohol or weed; it makes you very alert and sociable, I guess, but it can also make you feel very sexual to the ladies, depending on your personality." She blushed and turned to board the bus again.

The bus started to load up and was ready to move again. The driver was telling everybody to hurry up as he had a long drive ahead of him. Everyone got on apart from the young man who travelled from Mogadishu via Garowe to Las Anod, his family's city, who Mr Solution met 6 years earlier in Mogadishu.

The bus arrived in Burao around 8 pm, at the petrol station where they usually stop for rest and food until he continued the journey on to Hargeisa for another 3 hours. Mr Solution slung his bag over his shoulder and waved goodbye to the passengers he had shared that journey with, particularly Suleka, the Somali American girl, who normally would have been unloaded and invited to stay in Burao if he had an empty house. However, Mr Solution had to stay disciplined and focused as temptations could bring scandalous times one could not risk, so she smiled and waved back. "Take care, pretty young lady," said Mr Solution, who, instead of riding a waiting taxi, decided to walk home, stretching those legs after sitting for 6 hours in the bus.

He reached home that night, tired from the long journey, and decided to go to bed straight away, waking up the following day early to catch up with the local posse from Burao to find out what had been happening since he had been away for a few days. Then, after lunch, he would meet with those local authority officials and the sons of the local businessmen in the big mansion to discuss the trip, which they were eager to hear about. He would also try and find out who was causing all the trouble when he was travelling, as he was sure they would know or be the culprits.

It was almost 1 month until he was due to fly back to London after almost 7 years. Family members were always asking when Mr Solution was flying out. One was a 16-year-old boy, born in Somalia to a Somali British merchant navy seaman, who held a British passport got for him by his father before he died in Burao. He wanted to finally go to London and needed somebody from there to hold his hand until he reunited with other family members. However, Mr Solution was reluctant to take him along as he had places to visit in Ethiopia which were not appropriate for him. Also, he was anticipating political drama which could cause delays along the way; not ideal for the kid's journey. So, he said, "Kid, I will not take you, but just tell your mother to purchase a later ticket and I will collect you from the airport in London".

Some relatives who strongly disagreed with Mr Solution's political views and work, who resided in London, had been collaborating with the separatist regional regime of Somaliland employees to get Mr Solution out of Somalia, particularly the region they controlled, as he had become influential changing and nudging the status quo to the new political road map created by his visions and policies. These individuals had attempted to discredit and destroy Mr Solution, however, they had failed miserably, so had now decided to send him funds to purchase a ticket out of the country back to London, setting little traps along the way. However, these funds were sent over 4 months ago and he was still in Africa.

At lunchtime, Mr Solution met a friend from Sweden who had a farm on the west side of the city. He was cooking lunch of whole baby lamb, with fresh vegetables grown on his farm, to celebrate the completed construction of a solar-powered water rig to water his farm. He had invited Mr Solution and a few close friends to lunch, followed by the usual chewing of khat, in the same compound outside town.

The rest of the day was spent watching football on satellite T.V and talking about current affairs in the mansion. They were eager to find out about Mr Solution's trip to Garowe via Tukeraq and what he had done to stop the war there, as it had fallen silent with no fighting reported in the last few days. "I did what I said I would do before I left you, boys. You know, I don't just talk about it, I do something about it." He pointed at one of the guys sitting in the corner, who Mr Solution was convinced was behind the troubles on the way out. He'd had to take a swig from his water bottle as he nearly choked on the green chew chew, indicating it was all true what Mr Solution had just said. "I think you have help from Voodoo magic," he said, then Mr Solution got his mobile phone out and played the song "Superstition" by the legendry American soul singer, Stevie Wonder. "Do you understand what this song is about? Shall I translate for you?" Then one of the other guys said, "I know that song from my disco days in Mogadishu back in the days, man; fantastic song!" Mr Solution said, "The moral of the story is Allah helps who he wants that is with him. I thought you, always wearing that Arabic dress code, would know better, instead of talking about nonsense such as jinn or voodoo stuff."

The chap sitting in the corner also had several brothers living abroad in Europe. Two were in London, one close to Mr Solution's cousins who were women from his father's side. Also, his cousins from their mother's side of the family, whom they had completely brain-washed psychologically with fake political propaganda as they had economic interests from this separatist regime while Mr Solution had been away, fixing, nudging and shaping thinks in his country of birth. He knew when he returned to London there would matters waiting for him to sort out.

One of the guys said he was leaving to continue the session in another location and would Mr Solution like to join him? He agreed, and after a short drive to the edge of town, they came to a little hut with a small shop selling mainly khat, drinks and cigarettes. A woman was in the back making tea to for the few people sitting in her establishment. "Hey, lady, this is my friend. Organise a good sitting area for him, bring him more khat, sweet tea and whatever else he wants. I will return shortly as I have to visit somebody quickly," said the driver who had brought Mr Solution to this little shady-looking hut.

Mr Solution was sitting in the corner, minding his own business and feeling hot from all that khat. It was almost 11 pm and everybody had left except the lady of the establishment, two heavy loaded-looking lady friends and Mr Solution, who called the guy, but his mobile phone was switched off. Mr Solution asked the lady, who was now sitting in front of him smoking a fruity-flavoured tobacco shiisha with her lady friend, if he could have the bill so he could leave. She got up, rolling her long dress up to the middle part of her body, showing her enormous booty as she walked past. "Relax! We are going to be here for a while. I am sure your friend will return to pick you up. What's the rush?" Mr Solution leant back on the seating pillows but felt uncomfortable as this completely smelled like a trap, but he did not show it.

The lady fetched the little torch as this hut did not have electricity and was pitch-black, then sat back, grabbing the pipe to smoke. Mr Solution switched on the torch light on his phone and pointed it to the roof of the hut so he could get more visibility around the place. She then took her friend's mobile phone and started taking pictures between her friend's legs, discussing it in a way which made Mr Solution embarrassed enough that he got up swiftly to leave, moving five dollars into her account and turning right when he should be turning left towards his home. He wanted to get away from that area quickly as it certainly was a dodgy planned arrangement by the guy whose phone was mysteriously switched off.

A few weeks later, people were asking when he was planning on leaving to fly back after all these years. Mr Solution, who had two different bookings approaching soon, told one family member of one flight schedule, to which she said "Is it not the 25th of March?" which was correct. That told Mr Solution they had been going through his personal belongings in the house without permission, so he said, "I think you are right; I completely forgot." That week, the 5-bedroom house owned by Mr Solution was infested with blood-sucking bedbugs, so all the family had to leave for four days so the house could be sprayed with dangerous chemicals by a very strange-looking pest control man.

Mr Solution thought it was weird how these blood-sucking bugs had migrated to his house but none of the other houses on the street. Maybe it was a way to get him to leave this wretched place. Mr Solution took a small bag with important documents, buying essential needs such as T-shirts, boxing shorts and toothbrush from the town centre and checked into a 50-year-old hotel costing only a few dollars a night, which had satellite T.V and showers as the only luxury it provided.

For the next 4 days, Mr Solution had to eat all meals from outside in cafés and restaurants while the house was being sprayed by the pest control person, who informed the family the work could take longer than four days so they should not return as the chemicals were very hazardous.

Chapter 7.
The Journey Out

Finally, the journey out of Somalia via Ethiopia started towards the latter part of March 2019 with a four-hour bus ride to Hargeisa, then another bus journey a few days later of two and a half hours to the land border town of Wajaale. Then he rode a bus to Jigjiga city for 3 hours, staying for two days, followed by a plane ride to Addis Ababa airport to catch an international flight 24 hours later to London to have a meeting with a man who wanted to invest in a business proposition Mr Solution had created.

He woke up that morning to say farewell to family members and some young relative's children, particularly Sahra, who came from a rural nomadic countryside area to study in school in the city. He told them to keep learning, as a Somali proverb says, "aqoon la,aan waa iftiin la.aan", meaning "to be without knowledge is to be without light".

Then, shortly afterwards, he bought a ticket to Hargeisa. There was a one-hour wait until the bus fully loaded all the passengers and parcels, so Mr Solution decided to have one last breakfast in Burao, as he would be leaving for a long time after being in the city for more than five years. He went to a nearby restaurant and ordered an omelette and some tea with ginger and cinnamon. There was a man there with a fake smile who was part of a committee used by the local authorities in the province to silence dissent of individuals who had a different view against their political activities or policies. He was familiar to Mr Solution as they'd had several heated discussions on many different issues affecting the people caused by bad leadership, corruption, nepotism and having no real guts to do what's right for them. Mr Solution told him, "Your time finished long ago, old boy, but you failed to realise it the easy way, so, soon I think you will realise it when you feel the fire."

The bus was ready to leave as all were now on board. They passed through the same delightful scenery, stopping at boiling-hot Berbera port city for some drop-offs, pickups of people and to purchase some salted, chilli-flavoured grilled fish in takeaway containers from the local kids who boarded the bus to sell to passengers, finally arriving in Hargeisa in the afternoon. Mr Solution checked into the same hotel as last time. As he would be staying for 2 days and nights, he hoped to find the minibus driver who refused to pick him up as planned some weeks earlier to Garowe, due to paranoia and deliberate misinformation given to him, but he did not find him as he was away working.

The two days were spent socialising with the people of the city, including relatives, who were not supportive of Mr Solution's work due to conflict of interest on their part. One night, one of the relatives said, "I will pick you up from the hotel. We are going to dinner in an Indian curry restaurant. Mr Solution, who had been eating nothing but Somali cuisine all the time he has been in Africa, said "Hey, man, the last time I had Indian food was in London. Why did you not invite me there before?" This gentleman, who had moved from the UK for business purposes to Hargeisa, Somalia, laughed and said, "it's a new popular place, that's why!" After dinner, it was an early night for Mr Solution, who had a bus journey arranged for early morning to the land border trading town of Wajaale, between Somalia and Ethiopia.

At the bus station, he was surprised at the volume of buses leaving every half an hour to the border town of Wajaale. There was an extremely large Ethiopian population in Hargeisa, the second-largest city in the country, who entered without any proper immigration controls. This was a real concern to the local people who felt threatened by the sheer number of people coming in and out every day, and angry with their authority's failure to address the issue, whether it was the federal government or the separatist regime who administered it locally.

He boarded an overloaded bus, with the majority of people being Ethiopian migrant workers or traders returning, and arrived in the border town two hours later after driving on mostly rough roads on the Somalia side. Around midday, they stopped at a local money exchange place to obtain some Ethiopian currency to use on the other side of the dusty, rubbish-filled busy small town of Wajaale. Mr Solution had never seen this place before and thought it had serious economic potential, along with all other border towns such as Bali Janna / Barwaaqo, but it needed some serious development from both governments on both sides.

Mr Solution went into a restaurant for some food and drink on the Somalia side of the town, then walked to where the international land border of both countries was. With his leather travel bag over his shoulder and out of curiosity, Mr Solution, who had a mobile sim card from the Somalia side which was still active, decided to utilise it by checking where exactly the border line was using Google maps.

As he passed this little hollow area, he noticed lots of trucks stationed in both directions of the border. There were only two Somali policemen, armed with AK47s, on one side and many Ethiopian military army personnel a little bit further away, also armed, as the Somali region of Ethiopia had, in recent times, had turbulent political changes with a new government regionally and a new prime minister of the federal government with lots of civilian uprisings and thousands of deaths recorded between different ethnic groups and the government forces.

He was anticipating a large show of military force to be present, but as Mr Solution looked at his mobile phone, he noticed that some of the Ethiopian military were well inside the Somalia side of the international border. Not sure whether it was intentional or a mistake, Mr Solution said to the Somali policeman, "Do you know those Ethiopian federal soldiers are inside Somalia's territory? Are you aware of this? And as a border policeman, it's your job to know this and your gun is with you to use in defending the border; remember that!"

The policeman looked confused and did not reply. As Mr Solution continued to walk toward the Ethiopian side of the border, a young man approached him and said, "Do you want to go via the back way or the front?" Mr Solution said, "I am a front door man, so no!" As he continued to walk forward, looking for the place to catch the other bus to Jigjiga city, an Ethiopian military man called him over and said, "Documents." Mr Solution showed him his plane ticket and passport. "No visa; where is visa?" said the military man. Mr Solution said, "Where do I get a Visa?" He pointed in the direction of the Somalia side and after asking some people along the way, was told the Ethiopian visa from the Somalia side was requested, paid and printed in a printing shop after apparently communicating with the Ethiopian immigration department online, which was very unusual as this is the job of immigration officials normally, but as the National border and immigration department of the federal government of Somalia was not present at its own borders, unfortunately, due to internal political issues with the northern region of Somalia, this was the only option, so Mr Solution was asked to pay 70 dollars for a three-month Ethiopian visa.

He had to make a call to get some money transferred to his mobile wallet to pay for the visa from Hargeisa as, for some reason, he had completely forgotten about the visa costs and was only carrying just over a hundred dollars to use for the rest of the journey out. The funds were received straight away to his mobile phone then he paid for the visa, which was printed immediately. Behind him in the queue was very light-skinned, mid-forties or fifties Somali woman with a European passport (Danish or Dutch), also wanting a visa, who befriended Mr Solution as if she knew him in some capacity.

She said she was going to Jigjiga city on business and to see friends over there so recommended travelling together by hiring a private car to share the costs instead of taking the bus which she said was not very safe or comfortable, so Mr Solution agreed.

He walked together with Lucky, that was the name she gave, to the Ethiopian side of the border, passing a little rope in the middle of the road acting as a line of control. As soon as they crossed over to the Ethiopian side the smell is very different. The air was heavy with the smell of Ethiopian spices used to make their foods, however, 90% of the population were Somali Ethiopians, as this is their region of the Ethiopian land. They passed a little room where health checks for Ebola were done, as at the time, African countries were concerned about it due to an outbreak reported in the Democratic Republic of Congo, then another little tent where the documents were to be checked.

Finally, they moved further down the town where there were lots of bars selling Ethiopian alcoholic drinks such as beer and gin, which is very different from the Somalian side, where selling alcohol is illegal, although it comes through from Ethiopia as a contraband product sold illegally in Hargeisa.

There was a constant queue of trucks waiting at the border heading to Somalia. They were loaded with khat, which was considered legal in Somalia. It was the biggest export from Ethiopia, earning it more than a billion dollars annually, which had become a huge economic, social and health problem for Somalia. This made Mr Solution think that maybe legalising alcohol and making khat illegal would be less damaging to the people's health, particularly economically, as it was the most expensive commodity in the country.

Lucky stops at the bar opposite a gated one-floor building to speak with some people inside. Mr Solution sat outside and ordered an Ethiopian coffee to drink while he waited for Lucky. Two short men with moustaches sat at the table opposite, wanting to engage in some conversation but they didn't know where to start, so Mr Solution said, "Hey, lady, three more Bunna (coffees) please, anther one for me with one sugar and two for these fine-looking gentlemen over here." Mr Solution recognised, by their behaviour and dress sense, that these two men were Ethiopian plainclothes officers. They thanked him for the coffee. Mr Solution quoted a pan-African saying from Kwame Nkruma, the first president of Ghana, and how the security is performing in Ethiopia overall in the English language, then quickly, both men left the bar looking a little spooked, thinking this man was something a bit higher than their pay grade, maybe like a diplomat or something, which could cause big issues if they messed with him any further.

Within an hour, later Lucky emerged from inside the restaurant where she has been talking to some people who occasionally glanced outside, looking very suspiciously, and said, "This is my friend Americano. He will drive us to Jigjiga. Don't worry; relax, have a beer if you like. This is his car. Forget the bus you were going to travel in." He looked over and there was an old Toyota 4x4 with an Ethiopian number plate.

Mr Solution asked Lucky where he could purchase some khat for the journey, so she got hold of a young Somali boy and said, "Show him where mama sits". This confirmed that Lucky was very familiar with the town and its people, although she said she lived in Hargeisa and ran a beauty salon. A woman sitting under an umbrella at a table brought out a variety of different khats which were surprisingly expensive, considering Ethiopia is the producing country. A purchase was made of two high-grade quality bunches recommended by the lady. Mr Solution had made it a habit to chew this stuff whenever he was making a long-distance journey, particularly to an unknown place, as it made the journey seem quicker and more enjoyable and made him very alert to whatever was around.

The car pulled up outside the bar and bags were loaded up by this young man who worked in the border town, hustling to earn a living from the travellers who gave him tips for whatever work he did for them. Mr Solution asked the young man how he knew Lucky, as he seemed to know her. He mentioned some vague connections and the fact she was a regular traveller between Jigjiga and Hargeisa. There was a very drunk Ethiopian man who was fighting to get some money from Americano, the driver, and trying to stop them from leaving. Mr Solution called him over, told him to be quiet and gave him some money and suggested he get himself a whole flask of coffee to sober him up as clearly, he had drunk too much to handle.

Americano and his car finally started to move around 2 pm towards the road to Jigjiga. There were four people in the car - an Ethiopian man, who said he worked in Hargeisa as an Ethiopian consulate official, sitting in the front seat alongside the driver. The back seat was occupied by Ms Lucky and Mr Solution, who was getting his khat ready for the journey ahead. Just before leaving, a woman wearing a colourful dress approached Lucky's window asking for a lift. However, Ms Lucky flatly refused, saying we were full, although we had space for one more. Ms Lucky joked, "She is a big heavy-looking lady. I don't want to be squeezed by her and she might disturb the buzz from the khat. Give me some to chew." She was putting henna on and her hands were busy, so for the two-hour drive, they were having general conversations and listening to music, making sure Mr Solution was doing all the listening and not much talking, as he knew chewing the green stuff can make a person very talkative, and these passengers were on a mission of some kind.

Chapter 8.
Jamming in Jigjiga, Then Jetting Off

The Toyota arrived in the outskirts of Jigjiga in the early afternoon after a three-hour drive. It was the first time Mr Solution had visited this rapidly growing city, home to the Ethiopian Somali region's government.

Lucky said to the driver, "Stop by the newly built Love Housing Complex near the government buildings on the main road towards the city centre." This Love Complex had been funded and implemented by the previous regional government, then headed by Mr Abdi Omar, the regional president, who at this time, March 2019, was in an Addis Ababa prison awaiting trial for political and human rights abuse allegations.

This compound, with at least 30 red-tiled houses, was created and owned by the thirty couples married in what's been called the ending and integration of the long baseless illegal discrimination against certain communities. They were given a brand new 3-bedroom house, all wedding costs were paid, and they were given $2,000 cash to create sources of income for each couple by the previous leader of the region.

The car stopped outside a house on the main road surrounded by wide open undeveloped landscape on top of a hill with the city centre visible down below. Americano unloaded the luggage. Mr Solution stood at the side of the road having a cigarette break, then came over to Americano to pay him around 50 US dollars equivalent for the journey.

Mr Solution said, "Lucky, it's been nice meeting you but I should continue to the town centre with Americano to find a hotel for the next 2 night's stay before I fly out to Addis."

She shook her head and said, "You can stay with me at my girlfriend's house; it's all ready for you. Don't be silly. Let's catch a three-wheeler tik to the house.

"If you are sure and it's not an inconvenience to anybody, fine, let's go there to have some enjoyment." Lucky smiled then said, "Hey, stop that tik taxi!" Arms were waved at the rickshaw and the driver stopped sharply. Bags were loaded up, hen Lucky said, "Hey, you know where the Love Complex is around here?" He drove a little bit further down the road then said, "That's it on the right-hand side of the road." She told him to drive to the corner house with the little shop window where the bags were unloaded. The gates were opened by a housemaid and we were greeted by the lady of the house, who was a very attractive, tall meaty woman named Ubah. There was a strong frankincense smell coming out of the house. Lots of hugs and kisses were shared between Lucky and the lady of the house, then we were escorted to the living room which was arranged in a very relaxed way.

The lady of the house showed Mr Solution where he could have a quick shower using a bucket of cold water made ready, and the room where he could put his luggage, as he was expected to stay for the night. He really needed a quick shower as it had been a hot day and he had to freshen up after the journey.

The leather travel bag was taken back into the living room and placed in the corner as it had important documents and an object carried by Mr Solution in case he had to defend himself from any physical attacks. Then, he sat down, laying back on the cushions, wearing a traditional sarong for Somali men when they are relaxing at home or to be used as pyjamas to sleep in. The lady of the house had given it to him, saying that it belonged to her new husband as part of the wedding of the century. She added that he was away as he was a Somali businessman from Djibouti, trading in imports and exports from the two countries.

In the middle of the red carpet were trays of drinks, perfumes, burning frankincense, and cigarettes, along with the khat brought over by Mr Solution and Lucky, and an evening of getting high and sociable on the khat was well underway. Ms Ubah, who was sitting directly opposite Mr Solution, wearing a long colourful loose traditional Dirah dress, had incredibly large breasts, clearly on show deliberately by her posture and sitting position. This was starting to excite Mr Solution but he was a guest and the lady said she was married so he had to be on his best behaviour, specifically as it was Mr Solution's idea to intermarry the unjustly discriminated Somali tribes with the discriminators as a form of ending this backward, unjustified wrong history.

Ubah said she was from one of the discriminated communities and Mr Solution said, "It's absolutely absurd we Somali men have been deprived of such exotic beautiful women like yourself. I think we men are the ones who have been discriminated against, but credit where it's due to the former leader of the Region, Mr Abdi Omar".

The ladies liked this compliment and applauded, but Mr Solution had to be diplomatic as there was a new regional president of the Somali region of Ethiopia and the former leader had been arrested by the new federal government. Also, their headquarters were nearby and recently they had been hunting down the leaders and members of the former regime and if they thought he was a supporter or member of that former administration, they could arrest them.

Lucky was also a person Mr Solution was unsure of as she lived in Hargeisa but also said she had land and business interests in Jigjiga city, she was raised in Mogadishu and her parents were from a province called Awdal, and she said she was regularly visiting Jigjiga city when the previous administration was in charge, attracting Somali returnees from abroad who had investment capabilities.

She could also be a spy for the new Administration in the Somali region, or the Somaliland regime in Hargeisa, so Mr Solution kept it socially smooth while he was there, behaving like a person on vacation travelling on after few days, which was his plan anyway. Late in the evening, around 10:30 pm, the ladies said they would like some more khat, so Mr Solution went outside. It was completely pitch-black but the mobile phone had a powerful torch which was turned on. Travelling with a young boy who lived with the lady of the house and worked in a small shop by the side of the house owned by the family, Mr Solution, who was totally high on the khat and frankly, couldn't chew any more, walked to the main road with the kid to catch a rickshaw to town and back to purchase it quickly.

Around three am the following day, the session was finished so he went to sleep for a few hours before going to the city centre to be shown the sights by the girls, then, in the evening, to catch a short flight to Addis Ababa, then on to London the day after.

Because of the speed-like substance in the khat leaves, the household woke up late around midday to shower and have breakfast cooked early by the maid, then catch a rickshaw into the city centre.

He was surprised at the quality of the new roads created in the last few years by Chinese companies. The city was considered to be the fastest-growing city in Ethiopia, with many buildings under construction, lots of Ethiopian banks and shopping centres. The ladies left after showing Mr Solution around town. He entered the Buna bank to exchange some US dollars for Ethiopian currency so he could get a haircut from this very fancy-looking men's barbershop, then he had a late lunch from a restaurant inside a shopping complex where local T.V actors from the Somali region were sitting. Mr Solution greeted them, acknowledging that he knew who they were and said, "I like your comedy sketches; really funny stuff, guys. People watch it in Somalia from the region's T.V station, so keep up the good work!" Handshakes were exchanged then he went back to his table to eat lunch which had arrived by this time.

After lunch, he made a quick dash to the market to purchase some gifts, then he caught a rickshaw to the airport. Around 25 minutes later, the taxi dropped Mr Solution off just outside the airport checkpoint, manned by Ethiopian federal military guards, who, at that time, had taken over the security of the region as its local regional police force had been disbanded due to political conflict, bringing the takeover of federal security services.

Mr Solution was told the airport did not open for another two hours so he would have to wait here with the military man who had a Somali translator sitting with him. They all sat the grass under a tree for shade from the scorching sun.

The checkpoint officer was joined by a plainclothes officer wanting to check on Mr Solution who had arrived early for his scheduled flight. The plane ticket was shown to the officer who, after about an hour, said he could go and buy drinking water as he was very thirsty from all the chewing of the khat the previous night.

He walked a short distance to a tin shack just outside the terminal, which looked completely out of place as the Wilwaal airport terminal was brand new. The shack was boiling hot as it had a metal roof, but inside were seven military men and women lighting a charcoal fire to brew coffee.

Mr Solution ordered a bottle of cold water but the woman said, "no bottled water, no fridge, no electricity," so Mr Solution ordered a coffee and offered the military men some, but they declined the offer. Shortly afterwards, the airport terminal opened with people starting to queue outside the terminal. Mr Solution joined the queue where a woman asked him for a favour. "As you don't have any baggage except a carry-on bag, can you please take these two large suitcases on board for me to use your weight allowance as I will be charged extra otherwise?" Mr Solution declined for the second time, as there had also been another lady earlier on wanting somebody to carry a gift to somebody in Addis Ababa due to security reasons, particularly as there was a recent Ethiopian airline which crashed killing all passengers, but he said, "When we get to the check-in desk, I will ask if they will allow you to claim my unused luggage allowance as long as they know these suitcases are yours, not mine, with your boarding number on it."

Also in the queue was a short man with brown leather hand luggage, just in front of Mr Solution and, after a brief chat, said "I am taking these clothes for the new president of the Somali region who is in Addis Ababa. I am also his personal driver." Mr Solution was not sure what to make of this information or how best to use it as he only had around 8 hours until his next flight, so he said, "Please pass on my greetings to him from a fellow Somali brother".

Unfortunately, the airline check-in desk did not allow the request to transfer the unused baggage allowance of Mr Solution to the lady, as expected, so he proceeded to the security checking area and Mr Solution, who had left his cigarette lighter earlier in the bin outside, somehow mysteriously found it inside his leather travel bag along with another object he did not recognise, so he binned it again, directly opposite the security woman before going through the metal detector, telling her to pay special attention as he found this cigarette lighter which should not be allowed on airlines under laws introduced globally for safety reasons.

Mr Solution got the feeling there would be some drama attempted by individuals or governments wanting to cause inconvenience or frame Mr Solution for political reasons, so he knew he must be alert, calm and aware of any situation.

He moved on to the departure waiting room. The terminal had a single-plane runway, so there were no planes parked. An announcement said the plane to Addis Ababa would be landing shortly. A little later, a Canadian Bombardier jet-powered Ethiopian airliner landed, dropping off passengers, followed around half an hour later by the boarding of the travelling passengers. Mr Solution looked around the airport and fellow passengers as he boarded the plane. Two rows ahead in the queue entering the plane was a man with an Islamic-style flat hat who, some months before, inside a small supermarket owned by a young man of similar age from London, and again in a hotel called Ubah in Burao, had been acting very suspiciously or even paranoid as the shop owner explained at the time.

Mr Solution thought this man had been sent on some kind of a mission to follow him around from London to

Somalia and now Ethiopia because he kept popping up unexpectedly everywhere and when asked any questions, he acted in a very paranoid manner, eventually running away.

Passing along the plane's aisle towards the back row where his seat number was, he noticed, in the front seat, which might be first-class in a domestic short-haul flight, was seated a young Somali singer, named Hariir, from the Somali Ethiopian region. Mr Solution recognised him as his family members in Somalia used to always watch satellite T.V with performances from him and his Band in Jigjiga, so he shook his hand making him feel like a star as he was passing through to take his seat.

The plane took off from the airport runway with a minimal run-up and was very quickly already in the clouds, almost like a jet-engined military airplane. The flight duration was approximately one hour and fifteen minutes, and he had a conversation with a suited man, who changed seats with the passengers in front of Mr Solution, about the magnificent views below of mountains, dry-looking farming lands and cities. Then a massive water hole appeared, with water flowing in two directions away from it. Mr Solution said to the man in front, "Look down; the source of the Nile river is below us. It's a river full of history, always giving life to Allah's creations." The plane seemed to stay in the same position for almost five minutes, showing the great source of the

Nile river in Ethiopia which goes through several countries such as Sudan, before finally finishing in Egypt.

Ethiopia, at that time, had started the construction of a massive hydro-energy dam to produce electricity for its economy, with any surplus to be exported to neighbouring countries, giving it an economical boost. Mr Solution knew there was a dispute brewing between Ethiopia and Egypt, who said they would be affected by the filling of the dam as it would reduce the flow of water downstream, so, while in Somalia, he had discussed this with some government officials via unofficial channels, recommending the role Somalia would like to play was that of peace-broker by not taking sides. Hopefully, that would bring a successful resolution to the dispute as they did not want this issue affecting or destabilising the stability and economic recovery of all countries concerned.

Chapter 9.
The Trap in Addis Ababa Airport

The journey ended around 5 pm when the Bombardier jet landed in Bole airport and the next flight schedule to London was due to depart around 1 am, so Mr Solution, who had time to kill, decided to leave the airport terminal to catch a taxi to a place known as Bole or little Mogadishu in downtown Addis Ababa, to visit the Somali community conducting business activities in the Ethiopian capital.

The airport car park people were haggling with the drivers of some very old-looking taxis, some as old as 40 years, regarding the prices of the journey. A Somali woman approached to negotiate the price, then gave directions to the driver as she spoke the national language of the country.

She was also going to Bole area where her business was located, so offered to share the taxi with him. "Great. I would love to, thanks, lady," said Mr Solution. Driving through the city, Mr Solution noticed the new roads with fresh tarmac, road markings and tall blocks of flats, all being built by Chinese companies who were investing with many projects in the country.

The taxi stopped outside a tiny little shop selling ladies' products, where the lady got out. He waved goodbye to the lady then shortly entered a five-storey new building which was part hotel, part offices, with a restaurant downstairs where large crowds were sitting eating, drinking and watching English premiership football. Mr Solution ordered a drink with a little snack and was watching the football to pass some time before heading back to the airport to fly out to London.

Exiting the hotel building for some fresh air and a smoke, he was talking to the same taxi driver who brought him here earlier, arranging for him to take Mr Solution back to the airport. He happily agreed to, but completely overcharged the fare price, saying, "Give me all the Ethiopian money; you don't need it anymore. You are going home to nice rich London." So, Mr Solution gave it to him as a form of tip.

The driver dropped him off at the airport where there had been changes to the departure terminal. All of a sudden, airport employees outside were directing all international travellers to leave from the new terminal. When he entered the new terminal, where workers were still working on certain areas, he had to go through the initial check-in then through to the departures area with some bars open. Shops were still under construction, apart from a few finished ones, mainly selling Ethiopian cultural gifts.

The airport appeared busy as it was a connecting hub for the African continent and many airlines passengers transit to Ethiopian airlines to carry on their travels to various destinations globally. Mr Solution sat on a stool at one of the bars inside the departure terminal drinking a soft drink, waiting for the gate to be announced for flight number ET 700, when a young female waitress, who was very rude, with little grasp of the English language, told him, "Go, go", meaning you can no longer sit there waiting for the gate to open, although he had purchased a drink. Surprised at this rude girl's manners, he was calmly moving further down the terminal when the gate number appeared on the information screen. 'Good timing,' thought Mr Solution, who did not want to be there any longer and was looking forward to London after being away for so long. "Take me back to London," he said.

The queues for the departure gates were formed, Mr Solution joined the middle queue and noticed that the suspicious, sometimes paranoid man, who had been following him around, had joined the queue on the left just behind him, pretending he did not see him, although it was difficult to miss him. As the queue in the middle section was approaching the check-in counter for the flight, a man behind said, "Terrible airport this is, no WI-FI", making sure nearby persons heard him, so Mr Solution turned around and said, "Which country are you from?" He replied "Uganda". "So, does Entebbe have Wi-

Fi?" The queue moved forward. Waiting for the answer to the question, Mr Solution turned around but the man was no longer in the queue.

'Strange,' he thought, but as Mr Solution approached the counter, producing his passport and airline ticket, a young man named Johannes said, "Please wait over there for a moment." When Mr Solution asked him why, Johannes said, "Just some further checks".

Mr Solution waited in a seating area. By this time, most of the passengers had gone through to board the plane. An elderly, well-dressed woman reading a HELLO magazine, who said she was from Portsmouth, England but spent half the year in a house she owned in Cape Town, South Africa, asked Mr Solution, "Where are you from? And why are they keeping you waiting to board and not issued a boarding pass?" Mr Solution said, "London, and I'm not sure why; probably some silly wrong reason they will regret later on, but if they keep me back from this flight, do inform the good old British back home on your way there about a citizen who has been denied the right of passage in Ethiopia as he should be granted."

After a further conversation about football, Johannes came over, asking if Mr Solution had any further identification. Mr Solution said, "I don't know of better identification than a passport, particularly a British one, but let me search my travel bag." He searched the bag and found nothing except a passport-size photo of Mr Solution, who held it up and said, "Yes, I found a picture of me; look, it's me!" A group of young all-male American travellers started laughing at Mr Solution's comment.

All the passengers had boarded, including the dodgy guy from Burao who had been following him around. Only Mr Solution was sitting in the waiting area when Johannes came back with one of his colleagues who said, "The flight is now closed. We will put you on another flight tomorrow. Give me your passport and ticket." Mr Solution said in a loud tone, "I hope you have a good reason for this inconvenience and a decent hotel ready for me."

"Leave this area and return to the departure area; we will call you when we are ready." Mr Solution walked back to the departure area, wandering around or resting on these metal chairs, waiting for an announcement or for the supervisor to collect him as he had been waiting for 12 hours which was unacceptable.

Mr Solution was anticipating that some political opponents or primitive tribal-minded people or foreign countries had instructed the autocratic Ethiopian government or airlines to cause mischief for him while travelling through here as they thought he was a threat to their interests somehow. So, Mr Solution was calmly waiting for a call which never came.

The next day's flight had left and still no answer as to why he was being kept inside the airport without his documents or any explanation. Downstairs, on the lower floor of the departure terminal, was the counter for immigration issues or for people who missed their connecting flights to make arrangements. Mr Solution was at the counter asking to see the manager of the airport, or an Ethiopian government official, to demand an immediate apology and have a resolution to this fiasco, however, he was kept waiting, being told that somebody would come soon, but nobody came.

A young man with a heavy limp said he had travelled from South Africa on his way to Mogadishu, but had also been experiencing issues here for 4 days, living in the airport. Also, other passengers from Nigeria, South Africa, the Congo and Canada were all making inquiries. Mr Solution was tired of waiting and had spent all his money so had not eaten for almost 24 hours. There was no Wi-Fi available still at the airport. There was an internet café inside the departure building, but when he went to use it to get more information, he discovered it wasn't working yet. He remembered the man from Uganda's comment about this being the worst airport as it had no Wi-Fi, and now he fully agreed.

Mr Solution shouted at the girl at the counter saying that he had entertained this terrible situation and wanted to leave the airport until Ethiopian airlines corrected this error." The young lady came out to meet Mr Solution, informing him he could not leave the airport currently and giving him vouchers to buy food at the airline's lounges as often as he liked.

Mr Solution walked back up to the restaurant to eat. Just before he entered, he saw a man who used to be the governor of Burao who was travelling with a disabled child to Birmingham in the UK. He was looking very shady, sitting with two other men from southern Somalia; he was also a distant relative by tribe affiliation of Mr Solution, who clearly knew who he was but was pretending not to know him as he was a political foe of Mr Solution.

After eating at the same table as some Sudanese girls, Mr Solution went to a temporary prayer room on the other side of the departure lounge to perform the usual daily prayers, then decided to rest for a couple of hours on the little carpet inside the prayer room as he had not slept for almost 48 hours by now. After a much-needed short rest, while walking around the departure lounge, Mr Solution noticed a former minister of the previous regime in Hargeisa, nicknamed "bajaj", pretending to be asleep in the waiting area. Mr Solution stopped briefly in front of him, then laughed, saying, "Hey, bajaj, I am here!" He then returned to the immigration desk to ask for the management again, for the return of his documents and for them to immediately get somebody from the British embassy to the airport. The request was noted but the management appeared to be hiding from Mr Solution.

Passing through in transit were passengers from all parts of the world, particularly African countries, as Addis Ababa is home to the African Union headquarters. Three interesting passengers from East London, who were familiar to Mr Solution, passed through. They greeted one another and one of them said, "Your peace, unity and reconciliation building work in Somalia does not concern us in Hargeisa, so don't waste your time." Mr Solution had not seen these people for almost ten years but they were obviously aware of his work, keeping track of it online. It also appeared that they knew he was stuck inside the airport. "What are you talking about, hater?" was the response before walking away as he did not have the energy for this talk.

On the second day, still stuck inside the terminal, the airport Wi-Fi was finally connected, so Mr Solution posted on Twitter and Facebook, "Bole airport playing host to passengers from around the globe in the departures lounge".

He attempted to get some rest, although it was painfully difficult. A white South African man introduced himself and said that his family were the original Dutch Boer farmers and they became racist to black South Africans, such as Nelson Mandela, because of what the British did to them in the war. Mr Solution completely disagreed with this man as he was trying to justify the horrific crimes committed against the South African people by them, trying to blame the British as he knew the person he was talking to was British. "You will always have Nelson Mandela to fall back on when you are South Africans, as without his sacrifice, political leadership in letting the painful past go, reconciling, justice, liberating, unifying all South Africans, you would not have a country or business today. Remember that and excuse me; I am trying to get some much-needed rest."

He spent a second night at the airport, this time in a more comfortable flat reclining chair installed by the Chinese workers, who were standing around smiling towards Mr Solution, acting like Jackie Chan or something. The smoker's room was frequented by Mr Solution, who kept meeting interesting people from various countries, such as Saudi Arabia, Sudan, the US, China, Congo, Angola, Mauritius, Russia, and a short British man in a leather jacket, who paid attention to Mr Solution and those talking to him as if he was like a close protection officer of some kind. Maybe Mr Solution needed close protection as there had been these very dodgy meetings, to say the least, in the smoking room while he had been there.

After spending 2 nights and 2 days stuck inside the departure terminal, feeling tired and spaced out from lack of sleep, shower, food and with unprofessional Ethiopian airlines workers, Johannes called Mr Solution, saying there was somebody from the British Consulate here to see him. It was a young Scottish girl named Nicola and after a brief chat, she got Mr Solution's passport returned. Mr Solution demanded he be taken outside to a hotel room until they arranged a new flight, then a new flight was booked for 24 hours later. A minibus was arranged to drive Mr Solution to the hotel until the flight the following morning.

Mr Solution checked in then had a much-needed shower before catching up on some sleep, so that he could function well enough for a walkabout later in the evening and a meeting at another hotel called Harmony to obtain some information about certain people of interest.

That evening, during a 30-minute walkabout, Mr Solution was approached by pimps who said, "We have young university students you will like." Mr Solution did not understand initially but, after realising they were pimps, he said, "Not me and not today." A twenty-minute meeting at the back of Harmony hotel informed him of the person or groups who were behind his terrible customs issues, before returning to the hotel to have dinner in the restaurant, where a tall Arabic lady wearing strong perfume was sitting in front of Mr Solution with food in front of her but not eating. "You must be in love to lose your appetite, habibi", said Mr Solution. The lady smiled and said, "Does it show?" He nodded then went down to reception to arrange the shuttle bus back to the airport for an 11 pm check-in.

At long last, after three and a half days of unplanned stay in Ethiopia, the Airbus plane heading for London was in the air!

Chapter 10.
Landed in LHR

It was around 7 am when the Ethiopian Airbus touched down at terminal two in Heathrow after a tiring 8-hour flight. Due to the troubles encountered at Bole Airport all those nights before, Mr Solution was exhausted, but at least he had slept throughout the flight.

Sitting next to Mr Solution on the plane was a young, mixed-race, curly-haired woman who had travelled from Malawi, with whom he had a brief chat after returning from the plane toilet to brush his teeth using an airline toothbrush and toothpaste just before the plane was about to land in London Heathrow.

He exited the plane via the economy section, down the airport arrivals corridor, stopping to use the men's toilets. On leaving, Mr Solution bumped into the woman from Malawi who said she was travelling on to somewhere in southern England where she lived. She kept asking lots of questions regarding Mr Solution's time in Africa and what he had been doing while over there, however, some general short answers were given, then, as they approached immigration, they joined separate queues and that was the last encounter.

Mr Solution joined the queue sign-posted for Europeans with nothing to declare and attempted to use the automated self-service machine which could not read his documents, although it was a chip and pin passport Mr Solution was travelling with. He then returned to see a UK Indian-looking immigration official and presented his passport so he could go through. However, the man said, "Go and see the people over there." "Why?" asked Mr Solution, a little puzzled and showing some annoyance, especially after the horrendous time he spent at Ethiopia's airport. 'This was not the kind of reception I was expecting in my home city,' thought Mr Solution, 'especially after being away for so long doing tremendous work abroad. However, he approached the two women who introduced themselves as from the Metropolitan Police. They sat Mr Solution down in a waiting area. Next to them was an Ethiopian man and as they attempted to question Mr Solution, he said, "Can we go to a private room since you want to speak to me without these members of the public present?" pointing at the Ethiopian man. "Yes, sorry, this way please."

In a small room, the officers began asking some bizarre questions like, "What is your tribe?" Mr Solution couldn't believe the sort of irrelevant unusual questions being asked by these white British police officers. "Can I see your police badges again?" asked Mr Solution. "I just want to make sure you are who you say you are as this type of questions are ones I am used to in Somalia from Somali people who live in villages, not in the UK, unless I am dreaming and still in Africa."

There was a strong suspicion from Mr Solution that these police ladies had been deliberately misinformed, just as had happened in Addis Ababa, influenced by corrupt Somali individuals who didn't like him personally, or his brand of politics, or a dodgy foreign country such as certain Middle Eastern countries, wishing to cause problems as Mr Solution's policy had influenced the federal government of Somalia's decision to take a neutral position in a political dispute between certain gulf countries recently.

The women showed their police badges. Mr Solution took their police badge numbers and contact details. A man who said he was with security services came in and asked for Mr Solution's mobile phone, then returned a few minutes later to ask for the code which unlocks the phone. "I'm surprised you're asking this, but it's the shape of an S for Somalia." He smiles and left, then returned after a short while with the phone and said, "Very sorry; your free to leave; all good. We just had to run a random check. Here is your phone".

Mr Solution left this area of the airport via the arrivals entrance. Nobody was waiting to collect him as nobody knew when or where he was to arrive as the arrival was originally scheduled 3 days earlier, but due to the events and drama encountered in Bole airport, this was delayed by almost 4 days. So, he walked outside the terminal. It was the 30th of March 2019, still a little cold in London for Mr Solution who had been in the sun for 6 and a half years and was wearing a little polo t-shirt and brown Massimo dutti khaki trousers, purchased while in Africa.

Mr Solution was craving for a cigarette but had none and no sterling to purchase some. Then, a man who worked at the airport informed him there was a free bus shuttle service going to Bath Road to the Intercontinental Hotel. Mr Solution boarded the bus, getting off on the Bath Road, then had a 2.5-mile walk to Hayes town centre, a place familiar to Mr Solution as it had a high street with banks and shops.

Upon arriving at the high street, Mr Solution sat on a public bench and thought, 'W have I been doing all those years away, building a country and its nation?' Right opposite there was a Nationwide Building Society branch, and it just so happened that Mr Solution used to have personal accounts and a treasury account for the people's party of Somalia which he created while in London, so he went into the branch and spoke to a nice lady explaining that he used to have accounts but had been away for a long time so did not have bank cards or account details. With his passport as identification, she was able to trace the accounts, which still had funds available.

Mr Solution withdrew some money and went to the first newsagent, picked up the Daily Mirror and Telegraph newspapers then asked for a packet of 10 B&H. The lady said, "We only sale 20 packets; 10s are no longer being sold." That reminded Mr Solution that he had been away for a long time; much had changed in the country.

It was approaching 9 am, so Mr Solution, feeling nostalgic, entered a traditional British café and ordered a full English breakfast without the bacon and sausages and a strong cup of tea with two sugars, then sat in the corner looking at the domestic headlines in the newspapers before heading to the other side of London using the London transport system.

After a long breakfast in the café, it was almost 11 am. Mr Solution remembered the area well from all those years before and started to wander down the high street looking for an East African Somali restaurant he used to frequent on very rare occasions if in that part of London. thereafter a short walk, he found that it was still there but with a different trading name. He walked in with his bag over his shoulder. There were not too many people inside as it was early in the day. He had tea and little light snacks watching the news on a screen fitted against the wall showing the lively heated debates from the public and politicians regarding Britain's referendum vote to leave the European Union.

As Mr Solution was leaving the restaurant to continue his journey, a man from the same East African community with a familiar face entered. He looked shocked or spooked like he had seen a ghost at the sight of Mr Solution in front of him. After greeting him, Mr Solution headed to the nearest underground station to travel towards the northeast of London to pay a surprise visit to a special family member who Mr Solution had not seen for a long time.

He boarded the underground train heading northeast, sitting in the corner reading the newspaper as had always been the norm on the tube, but after a while of reading about current affairs, sports, culture and events, Mr Solution noticed that nobody was reading any newspapers as used to be the case, but everybody was glued to their phones or tablets. He felt a little embarrassed as if he was old-fashioned from the past, while these passengers were consuming information from their phones.

Around 2.45 pm, he arrived at the desired destination and sat around, admiring the view and killing some time until the person Mr Solution was visiting finished their day. Finally, at 3.30 pm, the person came out, greeted with hugs and kisses from Mr Solution, carrying a bag full of sweets, then he was escorted to their home. Everyone was very surprised at the unexpected visit. About 2 hours later, Mr Solution left to find some old friends then to book into a hotel for the night.

He booked into the Travelodge on the east side of London to recover from the jetlag of the long flight. The following day was spent purchasing a mobile phone with connection, shopping for basic needs then finally ordering a stone-baked pizza from the motel's bar. He then assembled the phone to make calls, trying to find old business and personal friends on the new mobile phone.

Next chapter. Work In progress!!!